Redleaf *Quick* Guide

Disaster Planning and Preparedness

IN EARLY CHILDHOOD AND SCHOOL-AGE CARE SETTINGS

Charlotte M. Hendricks
and Michele B. Pettibone

Redleaf Press®
www.redleafpress.org
800-423-8309

Published by Redleaf Press
10 Yorkton Court
St. Paul, MN 55117
www.redleafpress.org

First edition 2015
Cover design by Jim Handrigan
Typesetting by Douglas Schmitz
Typeset in Signo
Printed in the United States of America
22 21 20 19 18 17 16 15   1 2 3 4 5 6 7 8

Library of Congress Cataloging-in-Publication Data

Hendricks, Charlotte Mitchell, 1957-
  Red Leaf quick guide : disaster planning and preparedness in early childhood and school-age care settings / Charlotte M. Hendricks and Michele B. Pettibone.
      pages cm.
  Summary: "All adults who are responsible for the care of children should be prepared for disasters. This guide provides caregivers, educators, and program staff with preparation tips and step-by-step responses to disaster situations that are based on national standards and best practices to keep children safe"-- Provided by publisher.
  ISBN 978-1-60554-407-6 (paperback)
1. Schools--United States--Safety measures--Handbooks, manuals, etc. 2. Schools--Security measures--United States--Handbooks, manuals, etc. 3. School crisis management--Planning--United States--Handbooks, manuals, etc. 4. Emergency management--United States--Handbooks, manuals, etc. 5. Early childhood education--United States--Administration. 6. School management and organization--United States--Handbooks, manuals, etc. I. Pettibone, Michele B. II. Redleaf Press. III. Title.
  LB2864.5.H46 2015
  371.20973--dc23
                            2014033523

Printed on acid-free paper

CONTENTS

INTRODUCTION

Every individual responsible for the care of children may at some point be considered a disaster service worker and should be prepared to respond immediately and appropriately to disaster situations. Directors, managers, and owners of early childhood and school-age care programs are responsible for planning and providing training to staff members and volunteers.

The possibility of disasters has always been present. An event such as a tornado, fire, earthquake, or flood may have little or no warning leaving no time to prepare. An event such as a power outage, chemical spill, or act of violence may be isolated at your site or impact a community or neighborhood. Whatever the situation, the objective is to remain calm and take appropriate action to keep children and yourself safe.

This Quick Guide is written for early childhood and school-age programs, including family child care, center-based, corporate, Head Start and Early Head Start, pre-K, after-school care, and other programs serving children from birth to age twelve. It is designed to be a quick guide—a resource for caregivers and teachers to pick up and quickly find a reasonable response to a disaster situation. Directors and others can also use the book to train staff and volunteers.

This Quick Guide can help to

- identify disaster situations that may occur,

- prepare for emergencies, and

- respond to events.

Every program caring for children, regardless of the size or setting, should have a written disaster preparedness plan specific to their program and community. This Quick Guide is meant to supplement, not replace, that written plan.

There are three parts to this book. Part 1, Assess the Risk, helps program directors, family child care providers, and other caregivers prioritize planning and actions to keep children safe. Every disaster situation is unique; however, the basic initial responses involve evacuation or seeking shelter. Part 2, Respond to Disaster Situations, is for staff working directly with children. It lays out the steps to take in each disaster situation and is organized according to these responses:

- Evacuate

- Shelter

- Lockdown

- Drop, cover, and hold on

Space is provided for program staff and teachers to write notes specific to their disaster response.

Part 3, For Directors and Site Leaders, follows with information for program directors, staff members, and family child care providers to consider when developing and reviewing written disaster preparedness plans.

- Planning, preparation, and practice are essential, and help both adults and children to stay calm and respond appropriately.

- Be aware of the types of disasters that are most likely to occur in your community and geographic area and follow federal, state, and local regulations.

- Collaborate with local law enforcement, first responders, and Emergency Management Agency (EMA) personnel when developing and reviewing the written plan.

The book ends with a glossary of terms and a bomb threat report form that you can photo-copy and use at your program.

> In this Quick Guide, "program" refers to any early childhood or school-age care environment, from private family child care providers serving only a few children to large center-based organizations which may enroll hundreds or even thousands of children. "Facility" refers to any structure where children are cared for, such as a private residence, a center with several nurseries and classrooms, or a child care program within a large office building.

Part 1

ASSESS THE RISK

ASSESS THE RISK FOR A DISASTER EVENT

Most programs plan and practice fire drills and weather events (e.g., tornado). However, it is important to plan for all types of disaster events that might occur.

The risk of a specific disaster impacting a program may vary based on location, involving both geography and the community environment. The risk may also be related to an industry, a military base, or the transportation system, including railways, highways, and waterways. Review disaster events that have occurred in the area in the past, and consider events that may occur in the future.

Consider these examples:

- Fire, explosion, and wildfire

- Earthquake and landslide

- Tornado, hurricane, tsunami, and flooding

- Snow and ice storm

- Pipeline explosion and hazardous materials spill

- Power outage and transportation system breakdown

- Civil unrest, known criminal or violent individual in the area, and active shooter

> To learn more about the specific disaster risks, check the Federal Emergency Management Agency (FEMA) www.fema.gov website. The local emergency response agency (e.g., fire department) can also be consulted to identify the disaster risks for your program.

What types of disaster situation are more likely to occur in your community or geographic area?

_____

_____

_____

Part 2

RESPOND
TO DISASTER SITUATIONS

EVACUATION: IMMEDIATELY LEAVE THE FACILITY

Fire, gas leakage, carbon monoxide (CO) leak, explosion, or chemical spill in the facility requires immediate evacuation from the facility to the outdoor meeting place.

Immediately Evacuate If It Is Unsafe to Remain in the Facility

The time allowed to safely evacuate a facility after a fire warning sounds is four minutes or less.

Know the Warning System

The warning that indicates immediate evacuation is (describe):

_____

_____

_____

Prepare to Evacuate the Facility

Gather Children

- Infants, toddlers, and children with special needs may be carried or transported using an evacuation crib.

- Have children gather to evacuate. If two adults are present, have one in front and one behind the group.

- An evacuation rope with handholds (or other walking rope) may help children feel secure and facilitate evacuation.

Count Heads

- Check the room, including cribs, bathrooms, and closets, for children who may be sleeping or hiding.

- Do not delay—get children out of the facility.

- Notify the person-in-charge if a child is missing.

- Person-in-charge name/number:

Take Essential Supplies

Location of:

- To-Go Pack: _____

- Daily roster: _____

- Communication device: _____

- Medications: _____

Use the Planned Evacuation Route

- Feel the door before opening it. If it is hot, do not open it. (See instructions that follow for "blocked exit.") If door is *not* hot, exit the room.

- Follow the planned evacuation route. If a route is blocked by smoke, heat, or debris, use a secondary evacuation route.

- If there is smoke, have children "get low and go" by bending over while walking out.

Blocked Exit

- If possible, exit through a window.

- If trapped in the room:

  - Place a towel or blanket under the door to prevent smoke from entering the room.

  - Contact 9-1-1 or person-in-charge, if possible.

  - Make loud noises, such as banging on a wall. (Avoid yelling because it increases smoke inhalation.)

- Hang clothing or other object in or outside a window to alert first responders.

Go to the Outdoor Meeting Place

Go to the predetermined area where children and adults should meet outdoors, away from the facility.

- Location of outdoor meeting place: _____

- Count heads.

- Notify the person-in-charge if anyone is missing.

- Person-in-charge name/number: _____

Establish Communication

- Communicate with the person-in-charge.

- Wait for follow-up instructions.

- Do not return to the facility unless given "all clear" instructions.

Children's Learning Activity

Contact the local fire department and request they visit your program. In an emergency, children may be fearful of firefighters in full gear. It is recommended that children first meet the firefighters in their regular uniforms then watch the firefighters put on the emergency response gear, including breathing apparatus.

> Conduct regular evacuation drills. As children become familiar and comfortable with the evacuation procedures, vary drills so that children become familiar with two ways out. Also, hold drills at various times during the program day, such as during choice time or when eating.

EVACUATION: TO AN OFF-SITE LOCATION

Evacuate to an off-site location if the facility and campus are unsafe.

Evacuate to an Off-Site Location

The off-site location is a designated safe shelter such as a community center, library, or other public or private facility located away from your program campus. Evacuation may be directed by first responders.

- Potential flooding may require a planned evacuation from the program campus and transportation to a safe location.

- A nearby railway car collision or gas leak may require evacuation to a location several miles away.

Know the Warning System

The person-in-charge will notify staff members and direct evacuation procedures.

Prepare to Evacuate to an Off-Site Location

Gather Children
- Infants, toddlers, and children with special needs may be carried or transported using an evacuation crib.

- Have children gather to evacuate. If two adults are present, have one in front and one behind the group.

Count Heads
- Check the room, including cribs, bathrooms, and closets, for children who may be sleeping or hiding.

- Notify the person-in-charge if a child is missing.

- Person-in-charge name/number: _____

Put Identification on Each Child

Identification (e.g., wristband, tags) should be included in the To-Go Pack.

Take Essential Supplies

Location of:

- To-Go Pack: _____

- Daily roster: _____

- Communication device: _____

- Medications: _____

- Other (water, food, blankets, etc.): _____

Transportation

If Walking

- Count heads.

- Infants, toddlers, and children with special needs may be carried or transported using an evacuation crib.

- Keep children together while evacuating. If two adults are present, have one in front and one behind the group.

- An evacuation rope with handholds may help children feel secure and facilitate evacuation.

- Supervise children at all times. Continually count heads.

- Count heads again when the destination is reached.

If Transporting by Vehicle

Follow instructions of the person-in-charge to transport children.

- Count heads before boarding vehicle. Notify the person-in-charge if a child is missing.

- Load children on the vehicle. An adult should be on the vehicle and another adult on the ground to assist with loading. Count heads while loading.

- Buckle up all children in approved safety seats. Count heads.

- When the destination is reached, an adult should be on the vehicle and another adult on the ground to assist with unloading. Count heads while unloading.

- Check the vehicle, including under seats and in safety seats. Be sure no child is left on the vehicle.

- Follow instructions and take children to safe shelter. Supervise children at all times. Continually count heads.

Establish Communication

- Communicate with the person-in-charge.

- Wait for follow-up instructions.

> Follow the regular sign-in and sign-out process for children, whether on site or at a location away from the program campus. Keep authorizations and children's emergency contact information with you at all times. Check photo identification before releasing a child to the parent or guardian.

Children's Learning Activity

Show children photographs or a video clip of a home or building on fire or a wildfire. Tell them that sometimes fire gets too big and is hard to stop. Explain that while firefighters work to stop the fire, everyone else needs to get away from the fire so they will be safe. This might mean they go to another building where they will be safe.

BOMB THREAT

High-profile school violence cases and other national incidents, along with access to directions for homemade bombs on the Internet, have contributed to concerns about bomb threats and suspicious devices.

Communicated Threat

Threats may be delivered by telephone, cell phone, text, e-mail, website, social media, or other communication. The initial response is evacuation unless otherwise directed by first responders. Every situation is unique. Basic responses include the following:

- If a bomb threat is received, immediately contact 9-1-1 and notify the person-in-charge.

- If the threat is phoned in, try to obtain additional information. (See pages 85–86 for the Bomb Threat Report Form.)

- The person-in-charge initiates evacuation.

Know the Warning System

The warning that indicates immediate evacuation is (describe):

_____

_____

Prepare to Evacuate the Facility

Gather Children
- Infants, toddlers, and children with special needs may be carried or transported using an evacuation crib.

- Have children gather to evacuate. If two adults are present, have one in front and one behind the group.

Count Heads

- Check the room, including cribs, bathrooms, and closets, for children who may be sleeping or hiding.

- Do not delay—get children out of the facility.

- Notify the person-in-charge if a child is missing.

- Person-in-charge name/number: _____

Take Essential Supplies

Location of:

- To-Go Pack: _____

- Daily roster: _____

- Communication device: _____

- Medications: _____

Use the Planned Evacuation Route

- Follow the planned evacuation route.

- Be alert for any suspicious package or object. If an unknown or suspicious object is seen, use a secondary evacuation route. Avoid the area of the object.

> If a bomb threat is received, evacuate students to an area of safety away from the building. It is recommended that this be an area *different from the meeting place used for routine drills* because the explosive device (bomb) may have been placed where children typically gather.

Go to a Safe Area Away from the Building

- Count heads.

- Notify the person-in-charge if anyone is missing.

- Person-in-charge name/number: _____

Establish Communication

- Do not use cell phones or two-way radios until the "all clear" instruction has been issued.

- Communicate with the person-in-charge.

- Wait for follow-up instructions.

- Do not return to the facility unless given "all clear" instructions.

> To avoid triggering an explosion:
>
> - *Do not* move, touch, or handle unknown objects.
> - *Do not* activate alarms.
> - *Do not* use two-way radios, cell phones, or other devices.
> - *Do not* turn off lights or touch switches.
> - *Do not* make loud noises.

Children's Learning Activity

Show children an exit sign and explain what it is. Discuss how exit signs are located near doors that lead outside. Take a walk to look for exit signs and see where all exits lead. Help children understand that exit signs may look different (metal, paper, etc.), but that all have the same letters: EXIT (or other language).

Suspicious Package or Object

If a suspicious package or object is on site, the initial response is evacuation, as directed by the person-in-charge. Evacuation routes must avoid the area of the suspicious package or object.

If Suspicious Package or Object Is Sighted

- Move children away from the area.

- Immediately report the sighting to the person-in-charge. *Do not* use a cell phone, two-way radio, or other electronic device which might trigger an explosion.

- The person-in-charge evaluates the situation and calls 9-1-1.

Know the Warning System

Do not use a fire alarm, because different evacuation routes may be necessary to avoid the potential hazard. An announcement with specific evacuation instructions may be used.

Prepare to Evacuate the Facility

Gather Children

- Infants, toddlers, and children with special needs may be carried or transported using an evacuation crib.

- Have children gather to evacuate. If two adults are present, have one in front and one behind the group.

Count Heads

- Check the room, including cribs, bathrooms, and closets, for children who may be sleeping or hiding.

- Do not delay—get children out of the facility.

- Notify the person-in-charge if a child is missing.

- Person-in-charge name/number: _____

Take Essential Supplies

Location of:

- To-Go Pack: _____

- Daily roster: _____

- Communication device: _____

- Medications: _____

Use Evacuation Route as Directed by the Person-in-Charge

- This may not be the practiced evacuation route.

- Evacuation routes must avoid the area of the suspicious package or object.

- While evacuating, be aware of your surroundings. Be alert for suspicious objects and individuals with unusual behavior or actions.

- If something suspicious is observed, try to avoid that area.

Go to the Outdoor Meeting Place

- Go to the predetermined area where children and adults should meet outdoors, away from the facility.

- Location of outdoor meeting place: _____

- Count heads.

- Notify the person-in-charge if anyone is missing.

- Person-in-charge name/number: _____

Establish Communication

- Communicate with the person-in-charge.

- Wait for follow-up instructions.

- Do not return to the facility unless given "all clear" instructions.

> Always be aware of your surroundings, both indoors and outdoors. Be alert for and avoid suspicious packages and individuals with unusual behavior or actions.

Children's Learning Activity

Use games such as Follow the Leader to help children learn to listen, follow instructions, and stay with their teachers. It also helps to quietly sing a familiar song or chant to help children stay together while moving from one area to another. Practice the song and staying together during routine activities, such as going to the outdoor play area, as well as during disaster drills. This familiar routine can reduce fear and anxiety as you lead children to safety.

TAKE SHELTER (TORNADO AND SEVERE WEATHER)

Severe weather events, including tornadoes and flash floods, can occur quickly—sometimes with only minutes or seconds to respond.

Take Shelter If It Is Unsafe to Leave the Facility

A tornado or severe weather *watch* means weather conditions are right for a possible tornado or severe weather (e.g., wind, hail). Children should stay indoors and prepare to take safe shelter.

A tornado or severe weather *warning* means a tornado or weather event has been sighted or detected and is in the area. Immediately take children to the designated safe shelter.

Know the Warning System

Describe weather warning (e.g., tornado): _____

Prepare to Take Shelter

Gather Children

- Infants, toddlers, and children with special needs may be carried or transported using an evacuation crib.

- Have children gather to move to a tornado shelter. If two adults are present, have one in front and one behind the group.

Count Heads

- Check the room, including cribs, bathrooms, and closets, for children who may be sleeping or hiding.

- If outdoors, check the playground carefully, including inside playhouses, crawl-through equipment, and around bushes or structures.

- Do not delay—get children to safe shelter.

- Notify the person-in-charge if a child is missing.

- Person-in-charge name/number: _____

Take Essential Supplies

Location of:

- To-Go Pack: _____

- Daily roster: _____

- Communication device: _____

- Medications: _____

Use Planned Route to the Closest Tornado Shelter

Know the closest shelter.

- A closet or bathroom adjoining the classroom may be a safe tornado shelter.

- Every area of the facility (e.g., classrooms, cafeteria, hallways) should have a map posted that clearly identifies the location of the closest tornado shelter.

- Location of closest tornado shelter:

  _____

- Know the tornado shelter closest to outdoor play areas.

- Location of tornado shelter near outdoor play area: _____

In the Tornado Shelter

- Instruct children to sit in tornado safety position: sitting or kneeling facing the wall, with hands over the back of their heads and necks, and tucked into a ball.

- Place infants as low to the floor as possible. This may mean holding and covering the infant with your body.

- If possible, protect children with a blanket or other covering.

- Stay in this position until given the "all clear" instructions.

- Count heads.

- Notify the person-in-charge if anyone is missing.

- Person-in-charge name/number: _____

Establish Communication

- Communicate with the person-in-charge.

- Wait for follow-up instructions.

- Stay in the tornado safety position in the shelter until given the "all clear" instruction.

> If children are outdoors and a warning sounds, take children indoors to the closest designated safe tornado shelter (may be known as storm shelter).

Children's Learning Activity

Invite a local television or radio station meteorologist (weather forecaster) to visit the classroom and talk with children about safety issues related to weather conditions.

SHELTER-IN-PLACE (POTENTIAL ENVIRONMENTAL CONTAMINANT)

A possible environmental contamination *outdoors* may require shelter in a room that can be isolated and protected (i.e., sealed) from contamination until children can be safely evacuated. The person-in-charge will likely be informed of an environmental contaminant by first responders or other official. Instructions may be given to shelter-in-place until safe transportation from the area is provided.

Shelter-in-Place If an Environmental Contamination Occurs

Early childhood and school-age programs located in high-risk areas (e.g., near chemical plants or military bases) may have a specific warning system and response procedures in place.

Describe your shelter-in-place procedure: _____

Prepare to Shelter-in-Place

Gather Children

- Infants, toddlers, and children with special needs may be carried or transported using an evacuation crib.

- Have children gather to evacuate. If two adults are present, have one in front and one behind the group.

Count Heads

- Check the room, including cribs, bathrooms, and closets, for children who may be sleeping or hiding.

- Do not delay—get children to shelter-in-place room.

- Notify the person-in-charge if a child is missing.

- Person-in-charge name/number: _____

Take Essential Supplies

Location of:

- To-Go Pack: _____
- Daily roster: _____
- Communication device: _____
- Medications: _____

Go to Designated Shelter-in-Place Room

- Go to the closest shelter-in-place room. Location: _____
- If possible, follow planned route to the shelter-in-place room. To avoid hazards, alternative routes or instructions may be issued by the person-in-charge or first responder.
- Count heads.
- Notify the person-in-charge if anyone is missing.
- Person-in-charge name/number: _____

Isolate the Room from Contamination

The shelter-in-place room must be sealed against possible contaminants. Store isolation supplies at the designated shelter-in-place room. Location of supplies: _____

_____

- Cover windows, doors, ventilation vents, and other openings with plastic.
- Secure plastic with tape.
- Cover openings where air can pass through, such as around doors and windows, with tape.
- Keep children calm. Read a story or engage children in other quiet activity.
- Stay in the shelter-in-place room and wait for further instructions.

Establish Communication

- Communicate with the person-in-charge.
- Wait for follow-up instructions.
- Shelter-in-place until given the "all clear" instructions.

Store isolation supplies in the designated safe room. Basic supplies include plastic sheeting, wide tape (e.g., duct tape), and scissors. The isolation room should also have food, water, and other supplies necessary to care for children for several hours.

Children's Learning Activity

Young children learn by using their five senses: sight, hearing, smell, taste, and touch. When exploring the sense of smell, tell children that things like food, perfume, and flowers may have smells. Give children different items and talk about how they smell to them. Is it easy to smell or hard to smell? Do they like the smell? Experiment with different spices to smell. Discuss how sometimes you don't see the item, but you can smell it. The thing causing the smell might be invisible (e.g., a gas).

EXTENDED SHELTER

Situations such as flooding, winter storm, transportation system failure, and power failure could require extended shelter for children, staff members, and other adults. Parents may be unable to get to the program facility, and parents who do reach the facility may be unable to safely leave with their children.

Extended Shelter Is Necessary If It Is Unsafe to Leave the Building or Campus

Extended shelter may be mandated by the person-in-charge, first responders, or other Emergency Management Agency (EMA) personnel. The person-in-charge will provide instructions throughout the extended shelter time period.

Gather Children in Designated Shelter Area

The designated shelter area may be the children's regular nursery or classroom, or it may be a room they don't typically use. The shelter area may change at times during the shelter event. For example, children may remain in the classroom for story time or other activities, move to the cafeteria for meals, and gather in a gymnasium or other large room for physical activities and for sleeping.

Count Heads
- Count heads before, during, and after moving children to and from designated areas. Continually count heads at regular intervals.

- Notify the person-in-charge if a child is missing.

- Person-in-charge name/number: _____

Supervise Children
Maintain an appropriate child-to-staff ratio. Supervise children at all times.

Take Essential Supplies
Location of:

- To-Go Pack: _____

- Daily roster: _____

- Communication device: _____

- Medications: _____

Reassure Children

- Maintain a typical routine, including time for play, meals, and sleep.

- Discuss the situation with children in an appropriate manner. Assure children that their parents and families are safe and will get them when able.

- Distribute "comfort kits" for children, if available. (See pages 73–74 and glossary on page 81 for more about comfort kits.)

Use Supplies as Needed

It is recommended that programs have sufficient supplies to meet the needs of children and staff for at least one day (twenty-four hours). Supplies include water, food, blankets, and prescribed medications or equipment for children with special needs. (See pages 71–72 for more about supplies.)

Contact person on-site for additional supplies: _____

Location of supplies:

- Water: _____

- Food: _____

- Other: _____

Contact person off-site for additional supplies (if necessary), name/number: _____
_____

Establish Communication

The person-in-charge is responsible for organizing communication. It is essential that communicated messages be accurate and consistent.

- The person-in-charge will communicate with first responders and EMA personnel.

- The person-in-charge will communicate with staff members.

- Staff members should communicate with parents as instructed by the person-in-charge.

> Provide parents and families with regular updates using established communication methods.

DROP, COVER, AND HOLD ON (EARTHQUAKE OR EXPLOSION)

An earthquake or explosion may cause shaking and destruction. Such events often have no warning. The initial event may be followed by subsequent events that can cause further destruction and danger.

Take Shelter If in Potential Danger from an Earthquake or Explosion

Immediately take action at the moment of a loud, explosive noise. Drop, cover, and hold on. Take shelter immediately. Do not change location.

Know the Warning System

Signs of initial tremors may be observed, such as items on shelving rattling or beverages sloshing in their containers, or the first sign may be violent movement. Be prepared to take immediate action.

At the moment of a loud, explosive noise immediately take action.

During an Earthquake or Explosion

At the first sign of shaking or explosive noise, immediately do the following:

- *Drop* to the floor or ground.

- Take *cover* under a sturdy table or other furniture.

- *Hold on* to the legs of the furniture until the shaking stops.

- Stay away from windows and glass doors, fireplaces, and heavy shelving or appliances that could fall.

- Stay in place until the ground stops moving.

If Outdoors During Earthquake or Explosion

- Stay outdoors.

- Check the location. Move to an open area away from overhead objects that may fall (e.g., power lines, playground equipment, streetlights).

- Get down, gather children together, and have them sit with their hands over the back of their heads and necks, and tucked into a ball (i.e., tornado safety position).

- Stay in this position until shaking has stopped.

When the Shaking Stops

Assess and Prepare for Evacuation

- Look around for possible hazards. Determine if it is safe to move before getting up to help others.

- If indoors, decide whether to evacuate or stay in the current location.

- If outdoors, look around and avoid dangers such as falling debris or downed power lines. Go to the outdoor meeting place.

- Calm children. Count heads.

If in Immediate Danger

- Evacuate immediately if fire, damage to structure, gas leak, or hazardous material leak is detected.

- Go to the outdoor meeting place.

- Count heads.

If There Is No Immediate Hazard

- Check all children and adults for injury. Give first aid before evacuating.

- Do not move seriously injured persons unless there is immediate danger of further injury (e.g., fire or flooding). Instead, cover them with a sturdy table or other available furniture. Get medical help.

- Count heads.

Evacuate the Facility

Gather Children

- Infants, toddlers, and children with special needs may be carried or transported using an evacuation crib.

- Have children gather to evacuate. If two adults are present, have one in front and one behind the group.

Count Heads

- Check the room, including cribs, bathrooms, and closets, for children who may be sleeping or hiding.

- Notify the person-in-charge if a child is missing.

- Person-in-charge name/number: _____

Take Essential Supplies

Location of:

- To-Go Pack: _____

- Daily roster: _____

- Communication device: _____

- Medications: _____

Use the Safest Evacuation Route

- Use stairways (not elevators) and avoid windows and skylights.

- Be alert to the surroundings while evacuating the facility. Try to avoid falling debris, exposed wires, or ruptured gas lines.

- Be prepared for earthquake aftershocks.

If the Exit Is Blocked by Debris and You Are Trapped

- If there is no communication device available, or it is not working, make noise by tapping on something or whistle to alert others of the location.

- Avoid yelling and shouting, which could cause dust and debris to be inhaled.

Go to the Outdoor Meeting Place

- Calmly lead children to the predetermined area where children and adults should meet outdoors, away from the facility.

- Location of outdoor meeting place: _____

- Count heads.

- Notify the person-in-charge if anyone is missing or injured.

- Person-in-charge name/number: _____

Establish Communication

- Communicate with the person-in-charge.

- Wait for follow-up instructions.

- Do not return to the facility unless given "all clear" instructions.

After the earthquake:

- Be prepared for aftershocks, follow-up earthquakes that usually are smaller than the first one but can cause further destruction.

- Do not return to the facility unless given the "all clear" instructions.

- Inside the facility, be cautious of items that may have shifted and could fall from shelves or cabinets.

Children's Learning Activity

Show children dishpans, each filled with a different soil type (sandy, clay, topsoil, etc.) to examine. Ask the children to describe the texture, smell, and appearance of each. Ask children what uses the soil and encourage them to consider plants, animals, people, and structures. Let children add toy animals, plants, people, and structures to the containers. Tell them that sometimes and in some places the ground moves for a few seconds, and ask what they think happens to the animals, plants, people, and buildings. Allow children to shake the containers of soil and observe. Let children know that when the earth moves, it is called an earthquake and that it is an emergency. Everyone should "Drop, cover, and hold on!" in an earthquake. Encourage the children to practice dropping to the floor, taking cover under a table, and holding on while they chant, "Drop, cover, and hold on!"

LOCKDOWN

Lockdown is required for potentially violent or dangerous situations. The purpose of lockdown is to prevent access to children and adults. Examples of situations leading to lockdown are

- a noncustodial parent or an adult under the influence who wants to pick up a child,

- an irate staff member who could become potentially violent, and

- gunfire or an alert of a potentially violent individual in the nearby area.

Lockdown Means to Stay Where You Are and Away from Danger

Children should always be under adult supervision, including while using the restroom or changing classrooms. During lockdown, every adult is responsible for the children *under his or her direct supervision*. Immediately initiate lockdown in the current location (e.g., in the restroom).

Know the Warning System

If the potentially dangerous situation is outdoors or if there is an obvious threat, then use the most effective warning possible, such as an announcement of "lockdown" over an intercom system. However, if a situation is not yet an obvious threat (e.g., noncustodial parent), a discreet warning may be used to avoid escalating the situation. A hand signal or verbal code may initiate lockdown.

Prepare for Lockdown

Block Access and Reduce Visibility
- Close and lock the door(s) and window(s).

- Close curtains and window coverings.

- Turn off lights.

Gather Children

- Have children sit in the designated safest area of the room, preferably away from doors and windows or anywhere they could be seen.

Count Heads

- Check the room, including cribs, bathrooms, and closets, for children who may be sleeping or hiding.

- Notify the person-in-charge if a child is missing.

- Person-in-charge name/number: _____

Keep Essential Supplies with You

Location of:

- To-Go Pack: _____

- Daily roster: _____

- Communication device: _____

- Medications: _____

Lockdown

- Keep children quiet and calm.

- Read a story or have another quiet activity.

- Remain quiet in the safe place unless otherwise instructed. Be aware that a lockdown situation may become an evacuation situation.

- Do not return to normal activities unless given "all clear" instructions.

Establish Communication

- Keep noise to a minimum.

- *Do not* call out unless immediate assistance is needed.

- *Do not* use a telephone or other communication device unless necessary.

- Turn off ringer and lower voice volume on cell phones and devices.

- Be alert to any communication from first responders.

Be sure the lockdown warning reaches staff members who may be outside or on the playground with children. The adults and children may return to the facility, seek safe shelter nearby, or hide, depending on the appropriate response to the specific situation.

Children's Learning Activity

Play Simon Says and incorporate commands to stop, look, listen, and go. Make the game more challenging by adding commands such as "Quiet" and "Freeze."

ACTIVE SHOOTER

The goal of an active shooter is to kill people. An active shooter is a person who is actively engaged in killing or attempting to kill people, either on the campus or inside the facility. Active shooter situations are generally spontaneous, short time frame "killing sprees," ending within ten to fifteen minutes. Active shooters may also involve explosives and booby traps.

If an Intruder Is Seen with a Gun or Gunfire Is Heard in the Facility, Act Immediately

If possible, warn others of the danger.

If an active shooter is in the facility, here is how to respond:

- Get away (evacuate) from the shooter's location.

- Hide (lockdown) if safe evacuation is not possible.

- Fight—as the last resort.

It may be impossible to safely get away with young children. Hiding (lockdown) may be the only immediate option.

Get Away

Evacuate *only* if there is a clear escape route to quickly transport children to a safe area.

- Gather children and count heads.

- Check for children who may be sleeping or hiding.

Take Essential Supplies
Location of:

- To-Go Pack: _____

- Daily roster: _____

- Communication device: _____

- Medications: _____

Get Away If Safe to Do So!

For example, if the shooter is in another wing of the facility, escape may be possible through a nearby door or window.

- Exit away from the sound of gunfire and the shooter.

- Be alert for potential booby traps at exits.

Find a Sheltered Place Out of the Shooter's Sight and Line of Fire

- Lie down and get as low as possible. Comfort children and keep them as quiet as possible.

- Count heads. Take note of any missing children.

- Turn off sources of noise (e.g., cell phone ringers, radios, two-way radios).

- Quietly call 9-1-1 to alert the police of the shooter and your location.

> If escape is not possible, hide children in closets, cabinets, and bathrooms.

Hide

There may not be time and maneuverability to evacuate children in an active shooter situation. Hiding (lockdown) may be the only option.

Block Access and Reduce Visibility

- Close and lock the door(s) or blockade the door with heavy furniture.

- Lock window(s) and close curtains and window coverings.

- Turn off lights.

Gather Children in the Designated Safest Area

If possible, move away from doors and windows or where children could be seen. Place thick barriers (furniture, bookcase, etc.) between the windows and doors and the children.

Keep Essential Supplies with You

Location of:

- To-Go Pack: _____

- Daily roster: _____

- Communication device: _____

- Medications: _____

Hide

- Lie down and get as low to the floor as possible.

- Stay still and quiet. Comfort children and keep them as quiet as possible.

- Count heads. Take note of any missing children.

- Turn off sources of noise (e.g., cell phone ringers, two-way radios).

- If possible, quietly call 9-1-1 to alert police of your location. If the shooter is near, do not speak; rather, leave the line open for the dispatcher to listen. Turn the volume down on the phone.

- If the active shooter is close (e.g., immediately outside the door), keep children as quiet as possible. Be prepared to fight if necessary.

Fight

As the last resort, if your life is in immediate danger, fight to disrupt or incapacitate the shooter. Fight for your life!

- Be as aggressive as possible. You are fighting for your life!

- Go for the eyes, throat, or groin of the shooter.

- Throw things.

- Improvise weapons.

- Yell.

Follow Instructions from First Responders

Remember, law enforcement personnel will initially consider everyone to be a possible threat. When police and responders arrive:

- Keep hands visible in the air.

- Do not make sudden movements. Do not run toward police. Go toward a safe area away from the incident.

- Remain in the safe area until further instructions are received from an authorized individual (e.g., police).

Establish Communication after the Event

- Identify the person-in-charge. This may be a law enforcement officer or other authority.

- Communicate with the person-in-charge.

- Notify the person-in-charge of anyone missing or injured.

- Wait for follow-up instructions.

> If staff members and children are outside and hear gunshots, they should seek safe shelter nearby or hide.

Children's Learning Activity

Help children learn to follow instructions. Play the traditional children's game Red Light Green Light, a version of tag where children run when green light is called and freeze when red light is called. Playing this tag game without anyone ever being "out" increases the activity time for all and also contributes to fitness.

TRANSPORTATION EMERGENCIES

Disaster situations may occur while transporting children. Every early childhood and school-age care setting should have written policy and procedures for transporting children. Staff members should be familiar with and practice routine transportation procedures, including supervising children, loading and unloading, using safety seats (e.g., buckling up), counting heads, and other actions to keep children safe.

This section presents specific types of situations that may occur when transporting children to or from the program, and for field trips and other planned events. Examples of situations while transporting children include the following:

- The vehicle may break down or be involved in a collision.

- A road may be closed due to a traffic accident involving potentially hazardous materials.

- Flooding, snow, or ice may cause impassable roads.

- A tornado warning requires immediate shelter.

- An intruder may attempt to enter the vehicle or gain access to children.

In a Transportation Disaster Event, There Are Two Possible Initial Responses

- *Vehicle shelter-in* means to remain in the vehicle until help arrives.

- *Vehicle evacuation* is required if it is not safe to remain in the vehicle.

Establish Communication

This section refers to the person of authority on the vehicle as the "vehicle monitor."

- The vehicle monitor immediately establishes ongoing communication with 9-1-1 and with the program's person-in-charge.

- The vehicle monitor will instruct the onboard staff members and adults.

Vehicle Shelter-In

If the vehicle is safe, have children remain seated in the vehicle.

Count Heads
- Routinely count heads during shelter-in.

Monitor Children
- Check that children remain securely buckled up.
- Keep children calm. Tell stories and sing songs.

Communicate
- Listen for instructions from the vehicle monitor.

A vehicle shelter-in situation may change to a vehicle evacuation.

Vehicle Evacuation

Evacuate children if it is unsafe to remain in the vehicle.

For example, if
- fire is involved,
- the vehicle could be hit by oncoming traffic, or
- the vehicle is too hot (e.g., in hot weather).

Count Heads
- Routinely count heads during vehicle evacuation.
- Notify the vehicle monitor if anyone is missing.

Take Essential Supplies
- To-Go Pack: _____
- Daily roster: _____
- Communication device: _____
- Medications: _____

Follow Regular Unloading Procedures

- When unloading, an adult should be on the vehicle and another adult on the ground to assist children.

- Count heads while unloading.

- Check the vehicle, including under seats and in safety seats. Be sure no child is left in the vehicle.

Gather Children

- Count heads.

- Infants, toddlers, and children with special needs may need to be carried.

- Have children gather. If two adults are present, have one in front and one behind the group.

- An evacuation rope with handholds may help children feel secure and facilitate evacuation.

Move to a Safe Area

- Calmly lead children to a safe area, away from traffic.

- Keep children together. Be alert for children who may want to run or hide.

- Supervise children at all times. Continually count heads.

Communicate

- Listen for instructions from the vehicle monitor and from first responders.

Specific Transportation Disaster Events

Vehicle Breakdown

- Driver should move the vehicle to the side of the road, out of the way of traffic, if possible.

- Driver and vehicle monitor will assess potential danger to children.

  - Remain in the vehicle if it is safe to do so.

  - If breakdown includes fuel leak, fire, or other signs of danger, immediately evacuate vehicle.

Vehicle Involved in Collision

The driver and vehicle monitor will quickly assess the situation.

Minor Fender Bender

- Call 9-1-1.

- Count heads.

- Check everyone for possible injury. Children and staff members may be shaken from the impact. Administer first aid if necessary.

- Notify the program person-in-charge. Request alternative transportation or other instructions.

- Remain in the vehicle if there is no apparent danger (e.g., fuel leak, fire) and vehicle is not in danger of further collision. Evacuate if instructed by vehicle monitor or first responder.

More Serious Collision

- Call 9-1-1.

- Count heads.

- Check everyone for possible injury. Administer first aid if necessary. Do not move anyone with serious injury unless there is an immediate danger such as fire or flooding.

- Evacuate the vehicle because a serious collision has the potential for fuel leakage, fire, and explosion.

- Move children to a safe area away from the vehicle and away from traffic.

- Never return to a smoking or burning vehicle. Wait for first responders.

- Inform first responders and vehicle monitor of anyone missing or injured.

- Follow instructions of vehicle monitor or other authority (e.g., first responder).

Road Closure or Trapped in Traffic

Roads may be closed due to traffic accidents, hazardous material spill, or flooding. The vehicle may be rerouted or become trapped in traffic for an extended period of time.

- Remain in the vehicle if there is no apparent danger (e.g., fuel or chemical spill, fire).

- Follow instructions of first responders and other authorities. The driver may be rerouted.

- The vehicle monitor should contact the program. Inform the program person-in-charge of the situation; continually update him or her of changes in location and status.

- In the event of immediate danger (e.g., hazardous material spill or fire) the situation may require a vehicle evacuation (see above).

Weather Event

Sudden weather events can turn a routine transportation event into a disaster situation.

Wind, Rain, and Snow or Ice Squalls

- If conditions make roads impassable, the driver should pull off the road. Park the vehicle a safe distance from the road, out of the path of other vehicles.

- The driver should make the vehicle visible to other cars and rescuers. Turn on hazard lights and hang a bright cloth or flag outside the vehicle.

- Remain in the vehicle. Follow planned procedures unique to the area and season (e.g., use Mylar emergency blankets to retain heat in winter snow events).

Tornado, Visible from a Distance

- If a tornado is visible far in the distance, try to avoid its path by moving at right angles to the tornado's path.

- Turn on a radio for local weather reports and updates.

- The vehicle monitor should contact the program. Inform the program person-in-charge of the situation; continually update her of changes in location and status.

- Be prepared to be directed to a tornado shelter or other destination in the immediate area.

Tornado, Approaching and in the Immediate Vicinity

- If a tornado is approaching, and high winds and flying debris are present, the driver should park the vehicle immediately, at a safe distance off the road.

- *Do not* seek shelter under a bridge or overpass.

- If possible, the vehicle monitor should contact the program. Inform the program person-in-charge of the situation; continually update him of changes in location and status.

- Be sure everyone is buckled up.

- Cover infants and toddlers in safety seats with items such as blankets or clothing to protect them from flying debris.

- Have children and adults put their heads in their laps, below window level if possible. Cover heads with hands and a blanket or clothing.

- Stay in this position until the tornado has passed and winds have subsided. Then, complete the following:

  - Count heads.

  - Check everyone for injuries. Administer first aid if necessary.

  - Call 9-1-1 for assistance, if needed.

  - Contact the person-in-charge.

Assess the Situation

- If everyone is safe and the vehicle is operational, follow vehicle shelter-in procedures until further instructions are received from first responders or from the person-in-charge. Directions may be given to go to a tornado shelter or other nearby destination.

- If the vehicle is unsafe, evacuate. Damage to the vehicle may cause fuel leakage, fire, and explosion.

- Do not move anyone with a serious injury unless there is an immediate danger such as fire or flooding.

- Evaluate the surroundings to find the safest area, away from downed power lines, debris, etc.

- Move children to the safe area and wait for first responders.

- Inform the vehicle monitor and first responders of anyone missing or injured.

Flooding

- If transportation is necessary during a flood watch (flooding highly possible in the next twelve to thirty-six hours), keep alert for hazards such as rising rivers and streams, mudslides, and uprooted trees.

- If necessary, change the route to one of higher ground, away from hillsides and valleys. Avoid areas with high risk of flooding and other potential danger.

- Listen to a weather radio and a local radio station for information about flooded and closed roadways, and avoid those routes. Watch for barricades; turn around and find another route. Do not cross barricades.

- Do not drive through standing water. Turn around and find another route. Vehicles can be swept away in as little as a foot of moving water, and rapidly moving debris can disable a vehicle.

- The vehicle monitor should stay in contact with the program person-in-charge. Inform her of any route changes and continually update regarding changes in location and status.

Potential Violence

Suspicious Activity near Vehicle

Be aware! When loading and unloading children, be alert for individuals with unusual behavior or actions, such as a noncustodial parent who wants to pick up a child, an irate individual, or a person under the influence.

If suspicious behavior is observed, move children to avoid the individual. Have children remain in the vehicle, if possible. Call 9-1-1.

Violent Activity Outside of Vehicle

- Immediately lock all doors and close windows.

- Call 9-1-1.

- Move children away from windows, if possible.

- Have children get as low in their seats as possible and cover their heads with their hands.

- Stay in this position until the vehicle has moved out of danger or help arrives and "all clear" instructions are issued.

Suspicious Intruder Approaching Vehicle

- Immediately lock all doors and close windows and call 9-1-1.

- Remain calm.

- If possible, signal for help.

- Do not antagonize the individual.

- Be compliant and do as directed.

- Keep children as quiet and calm as possible.

- Wait for help.

> Program directors, drivers, and vehicle monitors should work with their transportation manager and other community resource personnel in advance to determine the best way to avoid and respond to transportation emergencies, such as flooding.

Children's Learning Activity

Create indoor and outdoor play areas to simulate traffic and pedestrian areas. Designate "streets and roads" on the playground or tricycle paths so children can practice both pedestrian and vehicle safety awareness.

Part 3

FOR DIRECTORS AND SITE LEADERS

PLAN AND PREPARE

This section provides information based on national standards and best practices for program directors to consider when developing and reviewing their disaster preparedness plan. Program directors should follow federal, state, and local regulations and work with local law enforcement, first responders, and other emergency personnel when developing and reviewing the written plan.

Develop and Review the Disaster Preparedness Plan

Every early childhood and school-age care program should have a written disaster preparedness plan specific to their program and community. Consult local law enforcement and other first responders when assessing the risk of specific events in your area.

Establish a Relationship with Community Public Safety Agencies

Work with local first responders and public safety personnel as you develop and evaluate your disaster preparedness plan. Provide a facility map showing classroom and nursery locations, and the number and ages of children in each room. First responders may be unaware of family child care settings and of early childhood and school-age care programs located within larger organizations.

Identify and work with the contact person for law enforcement (e.g., police chief, sheriff) for both emergency and nonemergency events.

- Invite law enforcement personnel to visit the program and share with children their role in helping to keep children safe.

- Describe warning alarms for the program, including those for evacuation, take shelter, and lockdown.

- Provide a copy of facility plans or blueprints showing entrances and children's nurseries and classrooms.

- Discuss community-wide evacuation routes in case of widespread emergency (e.g., hurricane).

Identify and work with the contact person for the fire department for both emergency and nonemergency events.

- Invite firefighters to visit the program and help children become comfortable with fire-fighters in full emergency gear.

- Review evacuation routes from each area of the facility.

- Provide a copy of facility plans or blueprints showing location of utility shutoffs and ventilation ducts to aid firefighters in the event of a fire.

Collaborate with the local Emergency Management Agency (EMA).

- Assess the risk of disaster in the community.

- Identify tornado shelters within the facility.

- Determine the safest room to protect children and adults from an environmental contaminant. Discuss supplies needed to isolate the room.

- Identify the most effective warning systems (e.g., smoke detector, NOAA Weather Radio) for the program.

Identify and work with local resources for transportation training.

- Identify available training resources or ask law enforcement personnel for recommendations.

- Provide training for vehicle monitors on what to do if an emergency occurs during transportation.

Be familiar with hospital and emergency health care services.

- Post the number of the Poison Control Center (1-800-222-1222) by each landline tele-phone; program cell phones with the number.

Maintain a System of Record Safekeeping

Protecting the administrative records of the program is vitally important before, during, and after a disaster situation. Child and staff member contact information must be current at all times. After a disaster, records such as enrollment information, insurance policies, and payroll records must be available or restored to continue operation of the program.

Two types of information are essential to the program's operation: business records and children's records. Business records include the legal and financial documents necessary for the program to operate:

- Bank records

- Insurance policies

- Personnel files

- Employee payroll records

- Facility rental or ownership records

- Inventories of equipment, furnishings, supplies, etc.

- Vendor contracts

- Tax documents

- Operating licenses

- Log-in and password information

Children's records contain information required to provide quality care; information may vary in scope depending on the size and type of program, and needs of individual children. Children's records include information such as the following:

- Emergency contact information

- Authorization

- Attendance records

- Teacher/caregiver reports

- Medical and special needs information

- Parent credit card or bank account information

- Social security numbers

- Social service case reports

- Court documents regarding children (e.g., custody)

Maintain Privacy Protection During a Disaster

The program must maintain confidentiality and keep information secure at all times. The disaster preparedness plan should detail methods to protect the documents (both paper and digital) and the information.

Protect Documents and Records

Every program should have a written policy and procedure detailing the proper method for organizing, maintaining, and protecting documents. Designate a reliable person to ensure the business documents and child records are regularly updated and secure. Examples of responsibilities may include the following:

- Regularly review emergency contact information for children and staff members, update as needed, and provide current copies for To-Go Packs.

- Inventory computerized and paper records that are essential to the operation of the program, and know the location (e.g., safe deposit box, computer file, file cabinet) and date of last update.

- Create regular backups of computer files, operating systems, and boot files.

- Establish a procedure to gather and transport mobile devices (e.g., laptops and tablets) during an evacuation.

- Regularly copy updated paper records and store copies in a secure, off-site location.

Computerized Records

Regular, routine backup is essential in case computer systems are destroyed or severely damaged. Without current backup files, the information stored on computers is gone forever when the computer is destroyed. Backups should include the operating system, boot files, and software used by the program, as well as data files. Backups may be created in-house by designated staff members or through an off-site computer service.

- If backups are saved to servers or on portable backup drives located at the facility, store additional copies at a secure location at least fifty miles from the facility. The backup copies may be electronically sent to an authorized remote computer or server, or a portable backup drive may be physically moved to the remote location. Establish a schedule (e.g., quarterly or semiannually) to regularly take updated file copies to the remote storage area.

- Backup copies can be loaded on mobile devices such as laptops, tablets, and smart-phones; keep these devices secure. Establish a contingency plan to secure computerized records in the event that mobile devices are lost. For example, install locator or "remote wipe" software on mobile devices.

- Privacy standards must be maintained at all times; backups should be stored at locations where the information cannot be accessed by unauthorized individuals.

- Off-site "cloud" backup services are also available to protect against the loss of records. Select a cloud backup service that meets current privacy standard requirements to ensure confidential information is protected.

Paper Records

Most programs have some paper records, such as applications, daily rosters, and visitor logs. Routinely copy and back-up essential paper files.

- Keep original legal documents and records that do not need to be accessed for day-to-day operations in a secure off-site location such as a bank safe deposit box. Seal documents in a waterproof document pouch before storing in the safe deposit box, because bank vaults may flood in events such as hurricanes.

- Make copies of documents necessary to the day-to-day operation, and store in a secure location at least fifty miles away. Seal documents in a waterproof document pouch and store in a dry area protected from insects and vermin. Establish a schedule (e.g., quarterly or semiannually) to regularly take updated file copies to the remote storage area.

Records Requiring Immediate Access

Some records must be readily accessible during a disaster event.

- Emergency contact information for children should be available in the To-Go Packs.

- Facility maps, blueprints, and keys may be required by first responders. These items should be carried in the Administration To-Go Pack. Or, pre-establish other arrangements with local first responders—ask about ways to quickly access these items.

- In some communities, the local police department keeps a list of programs caring for children.

- Ask if your fire department participates in the nationwide Rapid Entry System program. A Rapid Entry System program uses a secure lockbox mounted by a facility's entrance that can be opened by a master key or code held by the fire department. Check local ordinances, as some communities now require programs caring for children to use a rapid entry system such as Knox-Box, SupraSafe, or TRAC-Vault.

Designate Staff Roles and Responsibilities

The disaster preparedness plan should clearly identify the roles and duties of staff members. Designation of authority and responsibility helps ensure consistent messages and actions, and reduces confusion during a disaster event.

For programs with multiple staff members, clearly identify three people—by name and job title—who can take on the person-in-charge role, and rank them so it is clear who is next in line to make decisions if the first person listed is unavailable. The person-in-charge will

- work with first responders and EMA personnel;

- relay instructions from public authorities (e.g., first responders, law enforcement) to staff members and parents;

- communicate decisions for further action, such as to evacuate to an off-site location or to remain in shelter;

- determine if all staff members are accounted for (e.g., teachers, food service workers, maintenance personnel);

- arrange for transportation if needed;

- delegate responsibilities to others; and,

- coordinate communication with parents.

Program person-in-charge name and contact information:

First: _____

Second: _____

Third: _____

If the program has multiple facilities or sites, identify a primary contact person for each facility or site. This individual will coordinate with the program person-in-charge but also should have authority to make decisions as necessary to ensure the safety of all children and staff members at the facility or site.

On-site (facility) person-in-charge name and contact information:

First: _____

Second: _____

Third: _____

Delegate Responsibilities to Staff Members

Every staff member should know and practice his specific duties in a disaster event. Consider the responsibilities described below, and identify other responsibilities specific to your program. Remember, the primary goal is to keep children and adults safe.

Ensure Everyone's Safety

Teachers and caregivers are responsible for the children in their direct care. Planning, preparation, and practice will help ensure that all children are safe and appropriately cared for.

- Children must *always* be under adult supervision. Maintain appropriate child-to-staff ratios at all times, including during outdoor play, naptime, mealtime, and other daily activities.

- Teachers must take daily attendance and know where children are at all times. Count heads frequently throughout the day, especially when moving from one activity to another (e.g., going outdoors to play).

- Sometimes a child may be under supervision of an adult other than the regular teacher, such as when visiting the nurse or while using the restroom. If a warning occurs, each staff member is responsible for children in his or her direct care. For example, if an assistant is with three children in the restroom and the fire alarm sounds, the assistant should get those three children out of the facility to safety. The teacher is responsible for children who are with her in the classroom.

- In a disaster event, teachers must account for all children, counting heads and comparing that to the daily roster. If a child's location is not immediately known (i.e., missing child), the teacher must notify the person-in-charge or other person of authority.

- Likewise, the person-in-charge should account for all staff members—teachers, office staff, food service workers, and maintenance personnel—comparing names to the staff daily sign-in/sign-out system.

Gather Medications

If children or staff take prescribed medications, these medications and supplies must be available during an emergency. A twenty-four-hour supply of essential medications is the minimum to have in stock.

Assign the task of quickly gathering locked medication supplies and health care plans to specific, dependable staff members. Designate one person as "in charge of medications" and another person as "medications backup." During an emergency, follow these procedures:

- Medication must be securely contained and out of children's reach in a backpack, fanny pack, or other bag that is kept with the in-charge-of-medications person at all times. For easier transport, use two small, locked cases (such as locking bank bags), one for refrigerated medications and one for other medications.

- Use a freezer pack for refrigerated medication.

- Prescribed emergency medication such as epinephrine must always be immediately available to children for whom it is prescribed.

- Take medical supplies, such as syringes and nebulizers.

- Take a copy of children's health care plans and medical authorizations.

Turn Off Facility Utilities

It may be necessary to shut off utilities in the event of a gas or water leak, fire, or other event. Heating, cooling, and ventilation may be shut off if an environmental contamination occurs in the area. In case of fire, once the fire danger is eliminated, sprinkler systems may be shut off to prevent further damage. *Do not* disconnect cable or satellite TV systems. Available TV feeds may provide weather updates and other information. Find out if utilities can be shut off by program staff or if only the utility company has access. If staff members can access utility shutoff, then at least three individuals should know the shutoff location and procedures. Most facilities have main shutoffs for electricity, gas, and water utilities, and also for heating, cooling, and ventilation systems.

Planning for the emergency shutoff of utilities includes the following:

- Have up-to-date, accurate contact information for utility companies.

- Clearly identify utility shutoffs on a site map.

- If staff members can shut off utilities, make sure the locations are accessible and responsible staff members have access to a key (if locked) and necessary tools (e.g., wrench).

Utility contact information, site maps, and keys must be in a To-Go Pack. This pack must be readily accessible to the responsible person (e.g., person-in-charge) but in a location secure from other individuals, pranksters, or intruders. Consider giving a copy of the site map to community first responders or place a copy in a rapid entry system lockbox.

Establish Communication

Communication is essential in a disaster situation. For example, the person-in-charge must communicate with both staff members and first responders, and parents must be informed regarding their children's care. Facilitate communication by posting emergency phone numbers at every landline telephone, programming cell phones with emergency numbers, and informing first responders what channel will be used on two-way radios.

Select Appropriate Communication Devices

Communication indoors may be through a landline or intercom system. However, cell phones and two-way radios may be needed when staff members and children are playing outdoors, being transported, or evacuating to an off-site safe location. These devices should be included in the To-Go Pack for every event, including practice drills. The following questions are important to consider when preparing for a disaster or emergency.

Landline Telephones

- Can the telephone also be used as an intercom system? Does every classroom and nursery have a telephone unit?

- Does each telephone use direct dial-out to 9-1-1, or is it necessary to first access an outside line (e.g., dial "9")? Include stickers on each phone with directions for dialing 9-1-1.

Cell phones

- Is cellular service reliable in the area?

- Are staff members expected to use their personal cell phones? If yes, does the program reimburse for expenses?

- Is there a written policy and procedure regarding personal use (including texting) during work hours?

- Are cell phones fully charged each day?

Two-Way Radios

- What is the mile range for communication between radio devices (e.g., twenty to thirty miles)?

- Are batteries charged each day? What is the battery life when charged? Are additional batteries available?

- What channel will staff members use to communicate? If that channel is in use, what is the second frequency choice? Remind staff members that communication through two-way radio is *not* confidential.

Establish Your Communication Network

Clearly outline the communication that should occur in a disaster event and who initiates each communication. For example:

- Teachers must account for their enrolled children. A child may be away from his regular class and under the supervision of a different adult (e.g., a speech therapist) when an event occurs. Who does the adult with the child contact: the teacher or the person-in-charge?

- The person-in-charge must account for all staff members and visitors. Establish a "roll call" communication to account for all adults (and therefore children).

Plan How to Disseminate Information to Families

When children enroll, assure parents and families that their children are cared for every day and will be kept as safe as possible at all times, including during disaster events. Let parents know how they will be notified and updated in a disaster event.

- Remind parents to update their contact information, including cell phone numbers and e-mail addresses.

- During emergencies, the main contact number for the program should be answered by a voice-recorded answering service with information on when, where, and how to reunite children and families. Include the access code in your Administration To-Go Pack so the voice recording can be changed remotely.

- Find out if translators or special equipment is needed to effectively communicate with families.

- Consider group fast-fax, e-mails, and text. When setting up group contacts, be sure that messages do not identify or include information about individual children, staff members, or families. Group messages should not include names, cell phone numbers, fax numbers, e-mail addresses, or other information specific to individuals.

- Social media such as Facebook and Twitter can be useful in disseminating general information, but take precautions and avoid including identifying or confidential information or photographs of children. Local news and radio stations may also disseminate general information.

Have a Reliable Warning System

A variety of on-site warning systems can be used to quickly alert staff members, children, and families of a potential threat. A large center or a program located within a school or corporation may have an elaborate system of audio and visual alerts, with automated notification to first responders. However, a simple system of ringing a bell or using an air horn may be effective for a small facility.

Activating the Alarm

In almost all cases, the individual who observes the potential danger will initiate the warning system. For example, if a smoke detector goes off in a classroom, the teacher should initiate the facility-wide evacuation. Likewise, if a staff member observes an individual acting suspiciously, the staff member should immediately initiate lockdown.

Early Warning Allows More Time for Response

- Install and maintain working smoke detectors in every classroom and nursery and other areas as recommended by the local regulatory authority (e.g., fire marshal, state licensing department).

- Install carbon monoxide (CO) detectors as recommended by the local regulatory authority.

- Have a NOAA Weather Radio programmed for alerts in the local area. Place the NOAA Weather Radio in an area where it will be heard by a staff member.

- Sign up for text or cell phone alerts initiated by Emergency Management Agency, television and radio stations, and other community agencies.

- Note that community-wide warnings such as a tornado siren may not give sufficient time for action, one may not hear the warning, or the system may fail in case of power outage.

All warning systems and devices should be maintained and checked monthly. Replace batteries as recommended by the manufacturer. Electrical warning devices should have battery backup.

Reach Everyone with the Warning

- The warning system must effectively reach all staff members, children, and other individuals on the premises. This includes staff members and children who may be outdoors playing or moving in and out of vehicles.

- Familiarize staff members and children with each warning alarm's specific sound and required response. For example, the fire alarm (i.e., evacuation) might be the sound of a long bell ring, while the tornado warning (i.e., take shelter) could be a series of short bell rings.

- Some warning systems use a voice command, such as "Your attention, please. A fire has been reported. Leave the building immediately." If a voice message is used, it must be audible and clearly stated, and must use words understood by staff members and children.

Lockdown Warning

- If the potentially dangerous situation is outdoors, or if there is an obvious threat, use the most effective warning possible, such as an announcement of "lockdown" over an intercom system.

- If a situation is not yet a visible threat (e.g., noncustodial parent), a discreet warning may be used to avoid escalating the situation. A hand signal or verbal code may initiate lockdown without alerting the potentially violent individual.

- Be sure that staff outdoors (e.g., on playground with children) receive the warning and respond appropriately. (Refer to lockdown procedures on pages 30–32.)

Describe On-Site Warning
- Smoke detectors: _____

- Carbon monoxide detectors: _____

- Evacuate (e.g., fire): _____

- Take shelter (e.g., tornado): _____

- Shelter-in-place (e.g., environmental contaminant): _____

- Lockdown: _____

Plan and Prepare Evacuation

Situations such as fire, explosion, gas leak, or bomb threat require immediate evacuation. Other situations, such as earthquake or tornado, may require evacuation after the initial shelter.

- Maintain the required child-to-staff ratio at all times to ensure enough adults are available to safely evacuate all children.

- If the program cares for infants and toddlers, have evacuation cribs to quickly transport these youngest children. Evacuation cribs should meet Consumer Product Safety Commission (CPSC) standards.

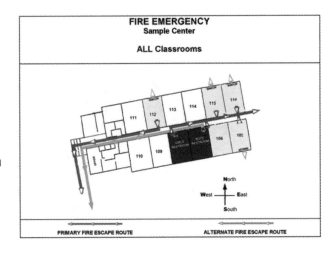

- Plan for evacuating children (and adults) with special needs (e.g., with wheelchairs).

- Plan for keeping children together. Children may not be able to see or hear the teacher when evacuating during a disaster event.

Evacuation Routes

- Every classroom, cafeteria, office, and other area should have two ways out. The primary evacuation route is through the closest door that leads outdoors and away from the facility.

- A window may be designated as an evacuation route if it will open wide enough for children and adults to pass through easily. Windows must be easy for an adult to unlock and open, must not be painted or nailed shut, and must not have security bars.

- All exit routes should have emergency lighting. Keep pathways clear of toys, furniture, equipment, and other objects.

- Exit doors must be unlocked or have a crash bar (also known as panic bar, push bar, and exit device) to immediately unlock the door.

- Each room and hallway needs a Fire Emergency evacuation route map that shows an accurate "You are here" label and the routes from that room.

- Indicate the primary evacuation route in one color and the secondary route in a different color. Be consistent in color coding for all maps.

- Evacuation routes must lead to an unlocked exit door that accesses an outdoor area where staff members and children can get safely away from the facility. Doors should be clearly marked EXIT.

- If a door leads to an enclosed area (e.g., indoor courtyard or fenced area with no escape), then clearly mark that door as NO EXIT.

- Evacuation routes must be accessible for wheelchairs, evacuation cribs (if caring for infants and toddlers), and individuals with special needs. Make sure doorways are wide enough, and install ramps as needed.

Outdoor Meeting Place

Designate an outdoor meeting place for each group of children. Always go to the meeting place when practicing evacuation. Familiarity with this meeting place will help children remain calm and allow the teacher to count heads more easily.

- Choose a meeting place that

    - is far enough from the facility to avoid immediate danger from fire and possible explosion,

    - is away from traffic and from where emergency vehicles will park, and

    - can be exited for further evacuation if necessary.

Many programs use an evacuation or walking rope for children to hold, such as the Grab & Go Evacuation Rope. The rope should be used during practice drills so children practice tightening the wrist straps and walking while holding on to the rope. As a learning activity, in a situation of smoke and heat, have children practice walking while bending over (i.e., *get low and go*) and holding the rope. Practice with the lights dimmed, and use a flashlight so children can see the reflective rope.

Plan and Prepare Shelter: Tornado

Severe weather and tornadoes can bring winds that reach three hundred miles per hour. These severe wind events can strike with little or no warning and may cause injury and loss of life in minutes. Choose a warning system (e.g., NOAA Weather Radio) that will provide the most advanced notice of danger.

A tornado *watch* means weather conditions are right for possible tornado, large hail, and damaging wind. If the facility is unsafe, such as a portable building, be prepared to evacuate to a safer area. A tornado *warning* means a tornado has been sighted or is indicated on weather radar. Immediately take shelter in the designated safe area of the facility. Do not leave the facility when a tornado warning is in effect.

Identify the Shelter Areas

Put as many sturdy walls as possible between children and the outdoors. A facility may have multiple tornado shelters to accommodate all children.

- Safe shelter areas are typically an interior hallway, room, or restroom on the lowest floor of the facility.

- Choose an area without windows and away from external doors.

- The area must be easily and quickly accessible and large enough to accommodate a group of adults and children.

- Remove glass and other items that could fall or become projectiles. Bolt shelving to walls.

- Post clearly visible Tornado Shelter signs at each shelter area.

Going to the Shelter Area

Tornado paths can quickly change, and tornadoes can touch down and "bounce" through an area. There may be only seconds to take shelter.

- Each room and hallway should have a tornado shelter route map posted that shows an accurate "You are here" label and the routes from that room.

- Exit routes and shelter areas should have emergency lighting. Keep pathways clear of toys, furniture, equipment, and other objects.

- Doorways and hallways must be accessible for wheelchairs, evacuation cribs (if caring for infants and toddlers), and individuals with special needs.

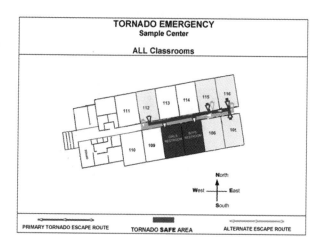

> Taking shelter for a tornado or weather event can be frightening for young children. You may be able to reduce children's stress by calling it a "weather hall party" (or other such phrase). Help children stay calm by telling stories or singing softly. Listen to a NOAA Weather Radio or other alert. If the threat is imminent, be sure children are in the tornado safety position.

Plan and Prepare Shelter: Earthquake

The risk for earthquake depends on location, with areas near fault lines at greatest risk. Earthquakes often have no warning, and aftershocks can cause additional destruction.

Make the Facility More Earthquake-Proof

- Bolt bookcases, shelves, and cabinets to wall studs.

- Place heavy objects on low shelves.

- Add lips to shelves to keep items from sliding off. Install latches on cabinet doors.

- Bolt down and secure refrigerators, water heaters, and gas appliances.

- Keep hallways and exits clear of objects that might fall and make evacuation difficult.

- Brace overhead light fixtures. Avoid hanging heavy pictures and other objects.

- Move beds and cribs away from windows. Avoid hanging mirrors, pictures, and other items over or near cribs and sleeping areas.

- Have a professional inspect utilities; repair or replace defective electrical wiring and leaking gas connections. Replace inflexible utility connections with flexible connections.

- It may be necessary to shut off electricity, gas, and water due to damaged and exposed wiring, a gas leak, or flooding. Know the location of and procedures to shut off facility utilities. (See "Turn Off Facility Utilities" on page 54.)

Drop, Cover, and Hold On

The objective is to prevent injury from falls, collapsing structures or falling objects. Immediately drop, cover, and hold on.

- If indoors, get under sturdy furniture, like a heavy desk or table, or against an inside wall, away from windows, mirrors, pictures, shelving, and other heavy objects.

- If outdoors, go to an open area, away from facilities, trees, fences, tall playground equipment, utility lines, and streetlights.

Plan and Prepare Shelter-In-Place: Environmental Contaminant

The risk of an environmental contaminant varies from one locale to another. Areas along major transportation routes (e.g., highways and railways) and heavily industrialized areas may have a higher risk of chemical spills. Communities located near refineries, nuclear facilities, or chemical plants may have established procedures that need to be incorporated into the program's disaster preparedness plan.

Work with the local EMA and other public safety agencies to assess the risk of an environmental contaminant. If a situation occurs with the potential for environmental contaminants, the recommended response may be to shelter-in-place. This means go to an area of the facility that can be isolated and protected from contamination and wait for instructions to safely evacuate.

Identify the Shelter-in-Place Location

- Select a room at the highest level above ground. Do not use a basement room. Hazardous gases often "sink."

- The room should provide a minimum of 10 square feet of floor area per person. For example: a room 10 feet x 10 feet could support 10 individuals (100 sq. ft. of room ÷ 10 sq. ft. per person = 10 people).

Prepare Isolation Supplies in Advance

The following essential supplies should be stored in the shelter-in-place area:

- Plastic sheeting (4–6 mm in thickness), precut and labeled for each window and door. Fold or roll up the labeled plastic sheets in correct order (beginning with first window and going around room).

- Additional plastic sheeting to cover ventilation ducts

- Duct tape

- Scissors

- Portable radio

- NOAA Weather Radio

- Bottled water

- Additional supplies needed to care for children until they can be safely evacuated (e.g., diapers and formula for infants, toys, games, and books to keep children quietly occupied)

Plan and Prepare: Lockdown

Lockdown is the initial response if a potentially violent or dangerous situation arises. Lockdown means to stay where you are—in a classroom, activity room, restroom, or other area of the facility. Move to the safest area of the room and take measures to protect children and yourself.

Evaluate the Facility

Invite local law enforcement to walk through the facility and help identify where and how an individual could enter the facility. If the program is located within a larger organization (e.g., business or school), determine how to prevent unwanted access to the children's area.

Exterior Doors

- Make sure every exterior door has a sturdy working lock to prevent unwanted entrance to the facility. The lock must allow for immediate exit in case of evacuation (e.g., panic bar).

- If keyless entry is used, only authorized staff members should have the code.

- Clearly identify a specific entrance for parents and visitors that is monitored by a staff member. Parents should sign in and sign out their children; and visitors should sign in and out.

- Many programs keep the main entrance door locked at all times, requiring a staff member to physically unlock the door to admit parents and visitors. Some programs unlock this door during scheduled drop-off and pickup times.

- Doors that open directly into enclosed play areas (e.g., fenced playground) may be unlocked while staff members and children are in that outdoor area. This allows immediate reentrance to the facility if necessary. The door should be securely locked after children and staff members return to the facility.

- Install alarms to indicate if a door is opened. This not only alerts staff members to potential intruders but also warns if a door is not completely closed.

- Walk through the facility regularly to make sure exterior doors remain locked (e.g., not propped open) and exits are clear in case of emergency.

Interior Doors

- Make sure doors to classrooms, activity rooms, offices, restrooms, and other areas can be quickly closed by pulling or pushing. For example, a teacher should not have to reach up and move a lever or prop to close a door.

- Deadbolt locks that can be quickly turned from inside the classroom (i.e., keyless thumb turn) offer security; administration can maintain a master key to access if needed.

- Locks should be secure, with the bolt entering a stud or sturdy door framing.

- Install locks in reach of adults but out of children's reach.

Windows

- All windows should securely lock.

- If windows serve as secondary fire escape routes, then barriers such as metal bars are inadvisable.

- Install window coverings that can be quickly closed to reduce visibility from outdoors.

Identify the Safe Area

Determine the area in each room that offers the most protection from an intruder.

- Reduce visibility from outside. Choose an area away from doors and windows. Move shelving and furniture to form an additional visual barricade.

- Put as many doors and barricades as possible between everyone and the intruder. A bathroom or closet with a locking door may offer additional shelter.

Plan and Prepare Off-Site Safe Shelter

It may be necessary to evacuate children to a safe shelter away from the program campus.

- A safe shelter often is a fire department, church, library, or other public facility.

- The safe shelter may be within walking distance or be several miles away.

- Establish a written agreement with the safe shelter site, and update the agreement annually, including contact information.

- The facility must be accessible during the program's hours of service. Many programs open early and close late in the day, and the safe shelter may not be open to the public at these times. Have the name and contact information (e.g., cell number) of individuals who can open the facility for children and staff members.

- The facility should meet the basic needs of children, including water and toilet facilities. Discuss availability of food, blankets, clothing, and other items to care for children, and consider storing essential supplies at the safe shelter.

- *Do not* tell parents the safe shelter location in advance. This security is to prevent abduction of children or other potential dangers that could occur in an unfamiliar and unsecured environment.

Transporting Children

Develop a plan to transport children of all ages and abilities to the off-site safe location. If walking to the off-site shelter, follow these procedures:

- Determine the safest route, considering safety when crossing streets, parking lots, and other areas with vehicular traffic.

- Plan methods, such as using evacuation cribs, to transport infants, toddlers, and children with special needs.

- Practice keeping preschool-age children together when walking.

If transporting to the off-site shelter, follow these procedures:

- Determine primary and alternative driving routes.

- If vehicles are readily available (e.g., program owned/leased vans), maintain a list of staff members who are trained and qualified to drive the vehicles.

- Identify community transportation resources. Establish agreements for provision of services.

Notifying Families

If time permits, leave a note on the facility door telling parents where children may be picked up. Be aware that the pickup location may be different from the safe shelter. Follow the program's guidelines for communicating with families. (See "Plan How to Disseminate Information to Families.")

Reuniting Children and Families

Follow regular policy and procedure when reuniting children and families at an off-site location.

- Only authorized adults may pick up children. Check photo identification of each individual, even if the person is known by sight.

- Check the identification of each child before releasing to an authorized adult. The child's regular teacher or caregiver may not be available to identify the child. Another option is to create a list of enrolled children with their photos; update photos frequently, especially for infants and toddlers whose appearance can change rapidly.

- Establish a policy and procedure for situations when the authorized person cannot pick up the child. This procedure may include telephone communication with the authorized person (e.g., custodial parent), or other arrangements.

- Protect children in every situation. A child may have information on file that indicates specific individuals who should *not* have contact with or pick up that child due to custodial issues.

Practice Regularly

Regularly practice disaster drills for disaster events:

- Evacuation (fire)

- Take shelter (tornado)

- Drop, cover, and hold on (earthquake or explosion)

- Shelter-in-place (environmental contaminant)

- Lockdown

The frequency of practice drills is based on the risk for the area and the program. For example, practice evacuation (fire) drills monthly, and conduct additional evacuation drills to familiarize staff members and children with secondary routes. Practice take shelter (tornado) drills monthly during tornado season. Lockdown may be practiced less frequently. Practice drills familiarize children with the warning sounds and appropriate responses and help reduce fear and confusion in an actual disaster event. Conduct practice drills in a manner appropriate for the children's ages.

Prepare Staff Members and Volunteers

All staff members and frequent volunteers should know how to respond to a disaster situation.

- Include disaster preparedness in orientation and training for new staff. Review disaster preparedness plans during annual staff training.

- Familiarize frequent volunteers with disaster response plans.

- As children become familiar with the procedures, conduct drills at various times during the program day, such as when eating.

Teach Children

Young children may become frightened by alarms and during practice drills. Use the practice drills to help children stay calm and learn to follow instructions for safety.

- Explain disaster situations in ways appropriate for children's ages. Do not frighten them; instead, emphasize there are ways to stay safe. Reassure children that they will be taken care of and they can help to stay safe by listening and following instructions.

- Know the children in your care well and predict how each child might react. For example, if a child typically will not stay with the group, then plan to hold that child's hand during evacuation. If the children are afraid of storms (e.g., thunder, lightning), pretend the tornado drill is a "hall party."

- Teach young children the individual actions of disaster drills in progressive steps. Begin with "stop and listen" to the teacher. As they master this skill, progress to the next step, such as gathering at the door.

- Use familiar games, phrases, and songs to guide children's actions. Games such as Freeze or Red Light Green Light help children learn to stop and listen. Follow the Leader helps children learn to evacuate calmly and quickly. Simon Says may teach lockdown response.

- Tell parents that children are learning about disaster preparedness and staying safe. Use take-home activities for parents to reinforce learning. Encourage parents to have and practice a disaster preparedness plan at home.

For more ideas on teaching young children about safety, see the book Safety *in the Growing, Growing Strong series by Connie Jo Smith, Charlotte M. Hendricks, and Becky S. Bennett.*

For parent information, see the book Hip on Health: Health Information for Caregivers and Families *by Charlotte M. Hendricks.*

Evaluate Practice Drills

Conduct unannounced as well as scheduled practice drills. During each drill, set clear expectations and evaluate the staff members' performance. Afterward, review the strengths and weaknesses of the emergency response with staff members.

Have Identification for Children

It is essential that children have identification tags (e.g., labels, bracelets) in a disaster event, especially if they may be evacuated to an off-site safe location. Consider these recommendations when designing children's identification tags:

- *Do not* put children's names on identification tags.

- Identification tags should include the name of the program, the city/state, and a contact number that can be reached even if the facility is damaged (e.g., fire, tornado). Consider using a phone number that can be programmed with a recorded response.

- Choose a type of identification tag that is easy to attach, will not easily come off, and will fit in the To-Go Packs. Avoid lanyards, neck cords, and pins.

> Self-sticking paper (e.g., Tyvek) wristbands can be preprinted with the program name and contact number and included in the To-Go Packs.

Supplies

Gather necessary supplies to provide quality care for children during disaster events. Prepack items in backpacks, wheeled totes, or other containers for easy transport. A lightweight backpack allows supplies to be easily carried, leaving hands free to assist children. Insulated backpacks can keep temperature-sensitive medications cool for several hours and allows the wearer to have hands free. Store the backpacks (or other containers) and supplies for immediate accessibility.

To-Go Packs

Essential items should be readily accessible to staff members in To-Go Packs for any emergency response, including practice drills. Supplies in the To-Go Packs allow teachers to meet children's immediate needs and help ensure the safety of children and themselves. Other To-Go Packs include those for medication and administrative needs.

Prepack as much as possible. Store the pack near the classroom exit door. Communication devices may also be located near the exit door. Items such as the daily roster and contact information must be readily accessible while assuring confidentiality. The following lists are recommendations and are not all-inclusive.

Classroom/Nursery To-Go Pack

- First aid supplies, such as those recommended in *Caring for Our Children*, 3rd edition

- First aid book, such as the Redleaf Quick Guide to *Medical Emergencies in Early Childhood Settings*

- Small LED flashlight with fully charged batteries

- Identification for children (e.g., wristbands)

- Communication device (e.g., cell phone, two-way radio) with charged battery

- Name and number of person-in-charge and other designated individuals (e.g., assistant teacher, bus driver)

- Contact number for first responders, law enforcement, and other community disaster resources

- Contact number for children's hospital or other medical facility and the Poison Control Center (1-800-222-1222)

- Reflective vest

- Whistle

- Evacuation rope for children to hold

- Facility maps showing evacuation routes, tornado shelter, and meeting place

- Directions to off-site shelter

- Permanent marker

- Notepad and pen

- Daily roster, to account for all children when counting heads

- Current contact information and authorization for each child

- Additional supplies required for children in your care, such as medications prescribed for children with special needs and formula for infants

- Other items based on local climate, such as Mylar emergency blankets for heat retention in cold climates or sun reflection in warm climates

Medication To-Go Pack

In the event of an emergency, necessary medications must be available to children and staff members. An empty Medication To-Go Pack should be stored near the medicine cabinet and medication refrigerator. If a warning occurs, the authorized person will retrieve medications from the cabinet and refrigerator and place them in the Medication To-Go Pack. The Medication To-Go Pack should never leave the control of the authorized person and must always be out of children's reach. The Medication To-Go Pack should be large enough to hold

- current contact information and authorization for each child,

- medical authorizations for children who have medications on site and dosage instructions, and

- necessary medications for children and staff members.

Administration To-Go Pack

Supplies in the Administration To-Go Pack include items and vital documents needed to continue the operation of the program when away from the campus, as well as basic emergency supplies to help ensure the safety of children and staff. These items should be readily accessible for every disaster response, including practice drills.

The Administration To-Go Pack should never be out of reach of the person-in-charge or the designee. The backpack or other bag should include a waterproof compartment for documents and have zippered closures that can be secured to prevent unauthorized individuals from reaching in and taking items. Prepack items such as maps, and store the pack in a secure but easily accessible location in the administration office. Communication devices may be located near the exit door. Items such as daily rosters, visitor sign-in sheets, authorization and contact information, and log-in/password information must be readily accessible while assuring confidentiality.

The following items are examples of recommended items for the Administration To-Go Pack.

- Contact number for first responders, law enforcement, and other community disaster resources

- Contact number for children's hospital or other medical facility and the Poison Control Center (1-800-222-1222)

- Facility map showing the classroom placement, room numbers, and number and ages of children in each classroom; evacuation routes and tornado shelters; and utility shutoff locations

- Current aerial photos of the campus, such as Google or Bing satellite map views

- Insurance contact information and policy numbers

- Log-in and password information to access online or cloud storage computer files, to remotely change the message of the facility answering system, or to send out text and phone alerts

- Master keys and other keys for doors, gates, and other lockable areas

- Directions to the off-site shelter and a copy of the written agreement

- Daily roster and sign-in sheet for staff members, children, and visitors to account for all persons on the premises

- Current contact information and authorization and identified photograph of each child and staff member

- List of all staff members' personal cell phone numbers

- First aid supplies and first aid book, such as the Redleaf Quick Guide to *Medical Emergencies in Early Childhood Settings*

- Small LED flashlight with fully charged batteries

- Communication device (e.g., cell phone, two-way radio) with charged battery

- Reflective vest

- Whistle

- Permanent marker

- Notepad and pen

Extended Shelter Supplies

Programs should have supplies to meet the needs of children and staff members for at least twenty-four hours. Work with local first responders to determine the risk of extended shelter situations. For example, programs located in remote areas not easily accessed may need to store additional supplies.

Use supplies as needed to care for children. Use what you need, and communicate with emergency personnel (e.g., EMA, first responders) to acquire additional supplies if needed. Do not ration drinking water for children or pregnant women. The following are supplies recommended for extended shelter:

- Water, at least one gallon of water per person per day

- Canned and other nonperishable food. Choose foods that the children typically eat. Avoid salty foods that increase thirst.

- Food for children and staff members with special food needs (allergies, diabetes)

- Infant supplies: formula, bottles, and nipples; baby food; disposable diapers in various sizes

- Food preparation supplies: manual can opener; disposable cups, bowls; disposable eating utensils

- Sanitation supplies: latex-free gloves; hand sanitizer; wet-wipes; paper towels; plastic garbage bags (medium and large); toilet tissue; and a bucket

- Fully charged LED flashlight with extra batteries

- Portable, multiband weather radio with extra batteries

- First aid supplies and first aid book, such as the Redleaf Quick Guide to *Medical Emergencies in Early Childhood Settings*

- Critical medications prescribed for staff members and children

- Blankets, one per person

- Extra set of clothing for each child, seasonally appropriate

- Child comfort kits (See pages 73–74 for more about these kits.)

Vehicle To-Go Pack

All vehicles used to transport children should have essential supplies on board and be easily accessible in the event of an emergency. Vehicles classified as school buses must include signage and emergency supplies as directed by national and local regulations.

The following lists are recommendations and are not all-inclusive.

- First aid supplies (See "Be Prepared to Administer First Aid" on page 74 for list of supplies.)

- First aid book, such as the Redleaf Quick Guide to *Medical Emergencies in Early Childhood Settings*

- Bodily fluid cleanup kit (to be used in the event of vomiting, etc.)

- Flashlight with fully charged batteries

- Communication device (e.g., cell phone, two-way radio) with charged battery

- Backup battery/charging source for cell phone or two-way radio

- Contact number for first responders, law enforcement, and other community disaster resources

- Contact number for children's hospital or other medical facility and the Poison Control Center (1-800-222-1222)

- Fire extinguisher

- Seat belt cutter

- Three red triangular roadside emergency reflectors

- LED battery–operated emergency roadside flasher beacons (*Do not* have traditional, flammable road flares on vehicles transporting children.)

- Extra batteries for flashlight and LED beacons

- Reflective vest

- Whistle

- Evacuation rope for children to hold

- Permanent marker

- Notepad and pen

- Other items necessary because of local climate, such as Mylar emergency blankets for heat retention in cold climates or sun reflection in warm climates

In addition, during transportation, the following information for each child should be on board:

- Daily roster, to account for all children when counting heads

- Current contact information and authorization for each child

- Additional supplies required for children in your care, such as medications prescribed for children with special needs and formula for infants

Child Comfort Kits

Comfort Kits are small packages containing items to help each child feel safe and comfortable in the event of an extended time of shelter. For example, programs located in colder climates may suggest extra clothing items in the event of a power or heating system loss, while those located in warmer areas may suggest instant cool packs and paper fans.

During registration, the program may ask parents to provide items for comfort kits to be given to each child in the event of a disaster situation. Individual comfort kits may be gallon-sized resealable bags filled with the children's comfort items that the teacher or caregiver carries in the To-Go Pack, or for older children, small backpacks that children can carry. Other programs may create group comfort kits for individual classrooms. Here are examples of items to include:

- Change of clothes

- Rain poncho

- Facial tissue

- Family photo or letter

- Small book

- Small stuffed animal or toy

- Warm socks

- Hat

- Paper fans

- Mylar emergency blanket

- Small nonperishable food item without nuts (e.g., cereal bars)

- Bottle of water

- Juice box

- Twelve-hour glow stick

Be Prepared to Administer First Aid

Injury can occur during a disaster event or practice drill. Most injuries are minor cuts, scrapes, bruises, and splinters. Less commonly, children may sustain serious injuries involving head injuries, broken bones, knocked-out teeth, poisoning, burns, choking, and drowning. Children also can experience medical emergencies such as severe allergic reactions to insect bites or food, and asthma attacks. Staff members and other adults present are also at risk of injury.

It is recommended that all staff members who provide care to children be trained in pediatric first aid and pediatric CPR skills. At least one staff person trained in pediatric first aid and CPR should be in attendance at all times with a child whose special care plan indicates an increased risk of needing respiratory or cardiac resuscitation.

Basic first aid supplies are mandatory. It may be most cost effective to use the first aid supplies (first aid kit) that are available for daily use. However, careful restocking of supplies must occur after each use.

Examples of First Aid Supplies (See *Caring for Our Children*, 3rd edition for full list)

- Disposable, nonporous, latex-free gloves

- Scissors

- Tweezers

- Non-glass, non-mercury thermometer

- Sterile gauze pads, flexible rolled gauze

- Adhesive strip bandages

- Bandage tape

- Triangular bandage and safety pins

- Eye patches or dressing

- Pen or pencil and notepad

- Cold pack

- Water to clean wounds or eyes

- Liquid soap, hand sanitizer

- Tissues, wipes

- Individually wrapped sanitary pads to contain bleeding of injuries

- Plastic resealable bags, garbage bags

- Telephone numbers of Poison Control Center (1-800-222-1222), children's hospital or other local medical facility, and emergency personnel (9-1-1)

- First aid book, such as the Redleaf Quick Guide to *Medical Emergencies in Early Childhood Settings*

- Cell phone or other communication device

RECOVERY AFTER A DISASTER

Throughout history, children have witnessed frightening events as a result of natural disasters or human activities. Children and adults can recover successfully and continue to have happy and healthy lives, but effective recovery requires the combined, supportive efforts of families and communities. Responsible adults in early childhood and school-age care programs play an important role in children's recovery.

Administrative Actions

Programs should have a plan for returning to regular operations after a disaster. Advanced planning such as establishing an administrative chain of command and protecting the business records of the program can ease some of the challenges of recovery.

Communicate

- Keep staff members and families continually informed and updated on program closure, hours of operation, and relocation. Maintain relationships with staff members, children, and families as you resume program operations.

- Communicate and work closely, as needed, with available community resources to facilitate the process of restoring the physical structure.

- Maintain regular contact with insurance companies and other resources to repair and replace the facility and furnishings.

Assess

- Conduct an inspection of the physical structure of the facility for damage. Contact appropriate agencies and experts (e.g., building department, structural engineer, health department) to provide inspections, recommend repairs, and authorize necessary permits to resume operation in the facility.

- Assess and itemize damage to computers, food preparation equipment, furnishings, classroom and nursery supplies, and other items.

- Assess the financial assets of the program. Financial obligations such as vendors' bills, payroll, and tax reporting must be met according to established timelines. Consider financial issues such as the following:

  - If the facility is closed for repairs, can the program meet financial responsibilities incurred before the disaster event?

- Are funds available to make necessary repairs to reopen the program?

- What is the time frame to settle insurance claims?

- If the event has been declared a major disaster, contact the Federal Emergency Management Agency (FEMA), the Small Business Administration (SBA), and other local emergency agencies for assistance.

- Develop a timeline for completion of cleanup, repairs, and equipment replacement. If necessary, determine both short-term and long-term timelines to relocate and rebuild.

Relocation

It may be necessary to relocate temporarily or possibly long term. If the facility remains structurally sound after the disaster, the program may be temporarily closed or relocated for cleaning and repairs. For example, repairs due to flooding from burst pipes or roof damage from high winds may be completed within a week or two, if supplies and qualified services are available. However, if repairs demand a longer period of closure or if the facility is destroyed, more permanent relocation may be required.

Program directors should work with community resources to secure a temporary or new facility to continue the program. Coordinate with child care licensing and other agencies to ensure compliance with state and local regulations.

Program services may be discontinued while the new location is being established. Some programs may not have the financial means to reopen or rebuild the facility. The program staff members may continue to work with the families of enrolled children to help them find quality care, either temporary or long term, to meet children's needs.

Resuming Operation

Once the facility is approved to resume operation by local governing agencies (e.g., building department, health department, licensing agency), the program administration should do the following:

- Restore business and child records of the program from backups, if necessary.

- Resume regular operating procedures. Avoid changes in schedules, procedures, or routines unless absolutely necessary.

- Provide information on disaster stress and methods of coping to staff members and families. Include contact information for community resources such as the Red Cross, community action agencies, and local faith-based organizations that offer assistance and support.

- Review the existing disaster preparedness plan. Address concerns and update procedures that may have changed due to a new facility location.

Helping Children

A disaster event can be traumatic for children. Although children do not fully understand what is going on, they may feel scared, insecure, guilty, sad, or angry about what happened.

Typical Reactions of Children after a Disaster

Children's reactions to a disaster event are individual; the severity of reactions may depend on their experiences during and after the event. Some children may have been exposed to extreme danger and may have personal injury or have seen others injured. Children may be coping with significant losses, including family, friends, and pets. Children may have witnessed physical destruction, including loss of their homes, favorite toys, and other belongings, such as security blankets. The way children see and understand responses of parents and other caring adults is very important.

Children may exhibit a wide range of reactions, and most children will be able to cope over time with the support and help of parents and other caring adults. However, recovery is a long-term issue; children may seem fine one day and then have problems later. Even very young children can retain memories of specific sights, sounds, or smells, and reminders such as strong winds or loud noises can trigger those memories. Some children may need counseling or professional mental health services to deal with severe trauma. Children process their experiences through play, so it is not uncommon for their play to involve acting out elements of the traumatic event.

A child's age affects how the child will respond to the disaster. The following presents examples of behaviors children may exhibit.

Infants and Toddlers

Infants and toddlers do not have the words to describe the event or their feelings. However, they demonstrate feelings through actions.

- Infants and toddlers may be irritable, cry more than usual, and want to be held and cuddled. They may seem to startle easily, act withdrawn, and fear separation from the parent or primary caregiver. Some children may display anger, excessive temper, and aggressive behaviors.

- Eating habits may change. Some children may have poor appetite, low weight, and digestive problems.

- They may have trouble sleeping and may experience nightmares. Sleep patterns, including naptime, may change.

- Toddlers may revert to earlier behaviors such as thumb sucking and bed-wetting. They may demand attention through both positive and negative behaviors.

- Some children may seem to fear an adult who reminds them of the event, such as the caregiver who was with them during the event.

Preschool-Age Children

Preschool children often feel helpless during a traumatic event, resulting in feelings of intense fear and insecurity. Although some preschoolers may also talk about their fears and feelings, many young children express their emotions through actions.

- Some children may cling, not want to leave the parent, and fear being left alone.

- They may demand attention through both positive and negative behavior. However, other children may be fearful and withdrawn, unable to trust others or make friends.

- Some children may exhibit anger, excessive temper, and aggressive behaviors. They may be verbally abusive. During play, children may act out the traumatic event, such as by breaking and throwing toys.

- Children may have difficulty sleeping both during naptime and at night. They may have nightmares, be afraid of darkness, and experience bed-wetting.

- Eating habits may change, such as loss of appetite and digestive problems.

Elementary School-Age Children

Elementary school-age children may experience a wide variety of behavioral and emotional symptoms following a disaster. The following list includes common reactions, and most children exhibit these or other responses for a short period of time.

- Children may demand attention by clinging, crying or whimpering, wanting to be fed or dressed, or competing with younger siblings for parents' attention.

- In some disaster situations, children have to perform adult behaviors during an emergency and cannot easily return to an innocent childhood. These children may then act older than their typical age.

- Physiological reactions may include headaches, nausea, complaints of visual or hearing problems, or persistent itching and scratching.

- Children may have difficulty sleeping, be afraid of darkness, and have nightmares or night terrors. Fear responses may be triggered by wind, rain, or loud noises. Some children may re-experience the disaster during play, dreams, or flashbacks.

- Social interactions may change, such as withdrawing from playgroups and friends; avoiding activities that remind them of the event; appearing to have difficulty feeling positive emotions. Children may also exhibit aggressive behavior toward adults or peers.

- Children may have poor concentration in school, experience a drop in academic performance, or refuse to attend school.

- Children may be saddened by the loss of prized objects or pets and fear they will be left alone or separated from their families.

Helping Children to Cope

After a disaster, if the facility is intact, this familiar area can provide children with a sense of normalcy. More importantly, the staff members, teachers, and caregivers can help children understand and recover after the event—even if the program has moved to an unfamiliar location. Routine and regular contact with teachers, caregivers, and friends helps children and families reestablish a sense of safety.

Teachers and caregivers play an important role in helping children understand and cope with thoughts and feelings about the disaster. Helping children recover and learn in the aftermath of a disaster requires creativity, flexibility, and adaptability.

- Be calm and reassuring. Acknowledge the loss, but discuss the community's efforts to clean up and rebuild. Assure children that family and friends will take care of them.

- Encourage dialogue and play enactment of their experiences. Listen to the children and allow them to talk or show about their experience. Share your feelings, too. As appropriate, teach words to describe their feelings. Allow space for questions. Listen carefully to the questions and answer honestly, providing only the amount of information you feel the child needs. Clarify misunderstanding about risk and danger, and reassure children that you and others will take care of them. Also, explain that you are helping them learn ways to stay safe (e.g., fire drills).

- Maintain daily routines and familiar activities. Provide activities that enable children to express their experiences and feelings both verbally and nonverbally. Incorporate a variety of projects such as drawing, stories, music, drama, and audio/video recording.

- Be patient. Acknowledge and reflect on what children say and do, and let them know their feelings are okay. Focus on their competencies, helping children identify what they have done in the past when they were frightened or upset.

- Focus on positive actions, such as discussing how adults are working to make things better. Involve children in actions to help themselves and others, such as making a card for someone.

Take Care of Your Own Needs

You will be better able to help children if you are coping well. Recognize and try to deal with your own reactions to the situation.

- Talk to other adults, such as family, friends, faith leaders, or counselors. Sharing feelings often makes people feel more connected and secure.

- Take care of your physical health. As much as possible, maintain healthy eating habits, be physically active each day, and get plenty of rest.

- Make time to do things you enjoy.

GLOSSARY OF TERMS

All clear: The signal given to inform that the emergency is over or is under control, and that it is safe to return to the facility and resume normal activities.

Bomb threat: A verbal or written notice that an explosive device is set to be detonated for the purpose of damage, injury, or death.

Bomb Threat Report Form: The form to be completed if a bomb threat is received, especially if by telephone. The form provides a checklist to obtain as much information as possible from the caller to aid law enforcement in identifying the type of explosive device and the caller.

Campus: The area of the program including the facility and surrounding grounds.

Carbon monoxide (CO): A colorless, odorless, and tasteless gas produced by the incomplete combustion of fuel. Carbon monoxide can be emitted if a heating system (e.g., furnace) is not working properly; it is also released through vehicle exhaust. It is highly toxic and can cause headache, dizziness, nausea, confusion, and even death.

Caregiver: The person responsible for the immediate care and safety of children. Caregivers may be teachers, other staff members, parents, or volunteers.

Comfort kit: A bag of familiar and helpful items to help calm and comfort children during an extended shelter event. A single comfort kit per class or individual comfort kits may be used.

Communication device: A cell phone, two-way radio, or other equipment used to maintain contact with staff members, the person-in-charge, and others.

Daily roster: The register parents sign each time they drop off or pick up their children at the program. This document provides the day's attendance information. It is also known as the "daily sign-in/sign-out sheet" or "roll book."

Disaster: Often called "emergency," this term refers to any event, regardless of the overall severity, that threatens the safety of children and adults.

Disaster preparedness plan: The document written specifically for the program, describing in detail the actions to be taken in the preparation of, during, and after an emergency or disaster at the setting.

Drop, Cover, and Hold On: The recommended procedure for protection during an explosion or earthquake: drop to the ground, get under a sturdy piece of furniture, and hold on until the shaking stops.

Emergency Management Agency (EMA): Each state operates a statewide EMA with offices located throughout the state, often with an office in each county. Other governing bodies including agencies in large metropolitan cities and American Indian tribal councils may operate an EMA. These EMAs follow guidelines of the Federal Emergency Management Agency (FEMA).

Essential supplies: Items that should be on hand at any time during a disaster event, including communication devices, critical medications, and the daily roster. Essential items are packed in a To-Go Pack.

Evacuation: The procedure to leave an unsafe area (e.g., room, facility, or campus).

Evacuation crib: Cribs with wheels designed to move infants and toddlers easily during an evacuation. Evacuation cribs should meet Consumer Product Safety Commission (CPSC) standards for crib safety.

Evacuation rope: A rope designed with attached rings, loops, or straps for young children to hold while walking as a group.

Evacuation route: The designated path to evacuate (e.g., lead, carry) children and adults to a safe area.

Facility: The physical building, or part of a building, that houses the program.

Federal Emergency Management Agency (FEMA): U.S. government agency whose primary purpose is to coordinate recovery responses to disasters that require resources beyond what state and local agencies can provide.

First responder: Persons such as police, paramedics, or firefighters who are authorized and responsible on the scene of an accident, emergency, or disaster.

Isolation supplies: Items necessary to seal the shelter-in-place room from air flow in the event of an airborne hazard. Basic isolation supplies include plastic sheeting, wide tape, and scissors.

Law enforcement: Agencies and the members of the agency charged with enforcing the laws and protecting the members of a community. These include police officers, sheriff and deputies, special agents, SWAT teams (Special Weapons and Tactics), and military police.

Lockdown: The procedure to secure the facility to restrict entry and access of a potentially violent individual.

Medications: Critical and prescribed medications kept at the facility for staff members and children.

NOAA Weather Radio: A radio receiver activated by the National Oceanic and Atmospheric Administration (NOAA) that automatically turns on to announce hazards and dangerous situations in the area. The most common announcements are weather advisories, watches, and warnings. NOAA radios also announce non-weather events, including natural disasters (e.g., earthquakes, tsunamis); technological disasters (e.g., chemical spills, nuclear plant emergencies), national emergencies (e.g., terrorist attacks), and Amber Alerts.

Off-site location: A designated location (e.g., public facility, church) that can provide shelter for staff and children if the program's facility is unsafe.

One-day/twenty-four-hour supplies: A stockpile of the items necessary to care for children and staff members in the program for at least one day in an off-site shelter.

Outdoor meeting place: A designated safe, outdoor location where children and staff members gather if the program's facility is evacuated.

Parents: In this Quick Guide, "parent(s)" refers to the adult(s) legally responsible for a child. This includes foster parents, grandparents, and other individuals given legal guardianship of the child.

Person-in-charge: The individual who has the authority to make decisions for the program in the event of a disaster. This person's responsibilities include communicating with public authorities (e.g., law enforcement, first responders), staff members, and parents; initiating emergency responses such as evacuation; arranging necessary transportation; and accounting for all adults and children who are part of the program.

Poison Control Center (also known as **Poison Center):** A medical facility that can provide immediate and expert treatment advice and assistance over the telephone in case of exposure to poisonous or hazardous substances. Free, confidential medical advice is available twenty-four hours a day, seven days a week by calling 1-800-222-1222.

Policy and procedure: A written document that describes in detail the rules, regulations, and actions to be taken during the day-to-day operation of the program.

Practice drill: Routine practices of the disaster response plan (e.g., evacuation, take shelter) to familiarize staff members and children with the procedure.

Rapid entry system: A secure lockbox mounted near a facility's entrance that is registered with the local fire department. The box is used to hold keys, facility plans, and other essential items. The fire department holds a master key or code to allow immediate access by first responders in the event of fire or other emergency situation. Rapid entry systems are required for commercial buildings by local ordinances in many areas of the country.

Safe location: An area evaluated to be safe for children and staff members in the event of a disaster. Different disaster situations may require different safe locations (e.g., tornado shelter, outdoor meeting place, off-site location).

Shelter-in-place room: The safest room in the event of an environmental contaminant. The shelter-in-place location is selected because it can be sealed off (isolated) from airflow from outside the room.

Take shelter: The procedure of remaining indoors in a safe room during a situation if leaving is unsafe or impossible (e.g., tornado warning).

To-Go Pack: A backpack or other easily carried container, prepacked with essential items. This pack is taken by the teacher/caregiver or other designated staff member if a disaster warning occurs.

Tornado safety position: The recommended physical position to protect from debris during a tornado or during an earthquake. Children should sit or kneel, with hands over the back of their heads and necks, and tucked into a ball.

Tornado shelter: The designated safest place to take shelter—the room or area most likely to withstand damage from a tornado and damaging wind.

Vehicle evacuation: The procedure to follow if the transportation vehicle is unsafe.

Vehicle monitor: The person-in-charge when transporting children by van or bus.

Vehicle shelter-in: The procedure to follow if it is unsafe to leave the transportation vehicle.

Warning system: The designated sounds and visual signals used to alert staff members and children of an emergency or disaster situation.

BOMB THREAT REPORT FORM

This or a similar form should be available at the main telephones in the program and be completed immediately after reporting the threat to the person-in-charge and/or EMA.

Questions to Ask

1. When is the bomb going to explode?

_____

2. Where is it right now?

_____

3. What does it look like?

_____

4. What kind of bomb is it?

_____

5. What will cause it to explode?

_____

6. Did you place the bomb? _____

7. Why did you put it in the building? _____

8. What is your address? _____

9. What is your name? _____

Describe Caller's Voice

- ☐ Male
- ☐ Angry
- ☐ Excited
- ☐ Slow
- ☐ Rapid
- ☐ Soft
- ☐ Loud
- ☐ Calm
- ☐ Distinct
- ☐ Slurred
- ☐ Female
- ☐ Stutter
- ☐ Lisp
- ☐ Raspy
- ☐ Deep
- ☐ Crying
- ☐ Disguised
- ☐ Nasal
- ☐ Accent
- ☐ Familiar

If voice is familiar, who did it sound like? _____

Exact wording of threat: _____

_____

<table>
<tr><td>

Background Sounds

☐ Street	☐ Animal sounds
☐ PA system	☐ Static
☐ Voices	☐ Music
☐ Motor	☐ House noises
☐ Local	☐ Office machinery
☐ Phone booth	☐ Long distance

</td><td>

Threat Language

☐ Well spoken (educated)	
☐ Foul	☐ Irrational
☐ Taped	☐ Incoherent
☐ Message read by caller	

</td></tr>
</table>

Time: _____   Date: _____

Length of call: _____

Number at which call was received: _____

REMARKS: _____

Receiver of call: _____

(Name and Title)

If a threat is received via text, e-mail, or website:

• Save the message on the system. DO NOT DELETE THE MESSAGE.

• Call 9-1-1.

• If possible, print copies of the message to turn over to the police and other EMA personnel.

RESOURCES

Books

Caring for Our Children: National Health and Safety Performance Standards; Guidelines for Early Care and Education Programs, 3rd ed., from the American Academy of Pediatrics, American Public Health Association, and the National Resource Center for Health and Safety in Child Care and Early Education. Also available at http://nrckids.org.

Growing, Growing Strong series by Connie Jo Smith, Charlotte M. Hendricks, and Becky S. Bennett. Redleaf Press.

Hip on Health: Health Information for Caregivers and Families by Charlotte M. Hendricks. Redleaf Press.

Making it Better: Activities for Children Living in a Stressful World by Barbara Oehlberg. Redleaf Press.

Medical Emergencies in Early Childhood Settings by Charlotte M. Hendricks. Redleaf Press.

Online Publications

Field Manual for Mental Health and Human Service Workers in Major Disasters from Substance Abuse and Mental Health Services Administration. www.store.samhsa.gov /product/Field-Manual-for-Mental-Health-and-Human-Service-Workers-in-Major -Disasters/ADM90-0537.

Guide for Developing High-Quality School Emergency Operations Plans from FEMA (Federal Emergency Management Agency). www.fbi.gov/about-us/cirg/active-shooter-and-mass-casualty-incidents/emergency-plans-for-schools.

Head Start Emergency Preparedness Manual from U.S. Department of Health and Human Services. http://eclkc.ohs.acf.hhs.gov/hslc/tta-system/health/center/ep/Head_Start _Emergency_Preparedness_Manual.pdf.

Websites

American Academy of Pediatrics: www.aap.org

American Red Cross: www.redcross.org

Caring for Our Children: www.cfoc.nrckids.org

Centers for Disease Control and Prevention (CDC): Emergency Preparedness and Response: www.emergency.cdc.gov/planning

Child Care Aware: www.childcareaware.org

Child Welfare Information Gateway: www.childwelfare.gov/management/disaster _preparedness

DropCoverHoldOn.org: www.dropcoverholdon.org

Federal Emergency Management Agency: www.fema.gov

FEMA Ready campaign: www.ready.gov

National Weather Service; National Oceanic and Atmospheric Administration; Weather-Ready Nation: www.nws.noaa.gov/com/weatherreadynation

US Department of Homeland Security: Active Shooter Preparedness: www.dhs.gov /active-shooter-preparedness